# CLASSIC *f*M

## FAVOURITE SHAKESPEARE

# CLASSIC *f*M

# Favourite Shakespeare

*Preface by Sir Derek Jacobi*

*Introduction by John Brunning*

## Hodder & Stoughton

First published in Great Britain 1998
by Hodder and Stoughton
A division of Hodder Headline PLC

A Hodder & Stoughton paperback

A CIP catalogue record for this title
is available from the British Library.

ISBN 0 340 73871 5

Typeset by Palimpsest Book Production Limited,
Polmont, Stirlingshire
Printed and bound in Great Britain by
Mackays of Chatham PLC, Chatham, Kent

Hodder and Stoughton
A division of Hodder Headline PLC
338 Euston Road
London NW1 3BH

# Contents

—ᴟᴟ—

# Classic FM Magazine Favourite Shakespeare Top 10

# Preface

## by Sir Derek Jacobi

Talent, luck, health, imagination and stamina (in whatever desired order) are essential qualities for the aspiring classical actor. The glory of Shakespeare's texts lies in their literary richness, profundity, universal truth and huge emotional range – an everlasting banquet for both actor and audience.

The vocal, mental, psychological and physical tunes to be played ensure that each performance is an orchestral journey of incredible demand and reward. There is no equivalent job satisfaction, buzz, thrill, call it what you will, to the challenge of winning over an audience, of compelling the spectator to listen, understand and share in the modernity, immediacy and universality of Shakespeare's art. It requires *all* an actor's skill – you can't 'short-change' Shakespeare.

He is for all times, all ages, all peoples – the plays defy absolute definition and thus every actor can imprint his own choices, personality and interpretation on them. They are the actors' university whose graduation day never dawns.

# Introduction

I owe a great debt to a lady called Mary Pratt, the English teacher who first introduced me to Shakespeare. I was twelve at the time and a pupil at Alderman Blaxhill School in Colchester. Miss Pratt had organised a school trip to see *Macbeth* at the now defunct Colchester Repertory Theatre.

Nobody, I suspect, would claim that their first encounter with the great man's work is easy. But even then, all those years ago, I was touched by the power of his language. It was a magical afternoon and the start of an enduring love affair with Shakespeare's work.

I was delighted to discover recently that the Royal Shakespeare Company now runs courses every year in which teachers and actors get together to discuss how to make Shakespeare more fun in schools. In this age of ever decreasing attention spans, it is vital that we find new ways to make learning about our greatest literary figure more attractive.

The characteristics of human behaviour Shakespeare describes are just as real today as they were in the sixteenth century. Take Macbeth and Lady Macbeth, for example. Throughout history, there have been countless examples of wives having to suffer weak husbands. And, as a parent myself, I can easily identify with the torments King Lear suffers over the behaviour of his daughters. But perhaps Shakespeare's greatest achievement is the way in which he portrays love in his plays and sonnets. Judging by our Top Ten, it clearly strikes a chord with readers of *Classic FM Magazine*!

If you still need convincing about Shakespeare's influence consider these immortal lines that we all know by heart: 'Once more unto the breach', 'To be or not to be' 'If music be the food of love', and 'Shall I compare thee to a summer's day?' – all fine examples of how Shakespeare has become part and parcel of our everyday language.

*Classic FM Favourite Shakespeare* is both a celebration and a 'taster' of the great man's work. To make it more interesting, we've woven the selection around the idea of the Seven Ages of Man. I hope you'll enjoy what's here and that it will encourage you to read and see more of these magnificent plays.

Finally, and at the risk of appearing totally fanatical, I'd like to propose a resolution. Every year on 23 April, Shakespeare's birthday, we should all read a bit of the great man's work *aloud* – to ourselves, or to anyone who'll listen. That should help break the drudgery of the journey to work! More importantly, at least once a year we can all share and delight in our greatest poet, who is, as Derek Jacobi says, 'For all times, all ages, all peoples.'

# SEVEN AGES OF MAN

All the world's a stage,
And all the men and women merely players.
They have their exits and their entrances,
And one man in his time plays many parts,
His acts being seven ages.

# As You Like It

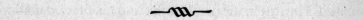

There can be no doubt that Shakespeare had a unique understanding of people. So what better way to appreciate and enjoy his work than through the characters he created? The fascination of Hamlet and his preoccupation with the nature of free will; the complexity of Falstaff, the epitome of the self-indulgent braggart; the unbelievable evil of Richard III whose soul was as deformed as his body.

In Jaques' speech from *As You Like It*, Shakespeare himself has given us the ideal outline for exploring the make-up and motivations of some of his characters in greater depth, identifying them as he does by those seven ages that constitute our allotted span.

Jaques himself – a philosophical, contemplative and melancholy idler – actually has little to do with the plot of *As You Like It*. His musings, however, are among Shakespeare's most frequently quoted lines.

By the start of the play, Duke Frederick has banished the rightful Duke, Rosalind's father, to the Forest of Arden where he is attended by Jaques. Orlando, whom Rosalind met at a contest in which he beat the Duke's wrestler, has also fled to the forest. At this moment in the plot, the two men have just met for the first time.

## Act 2, Scene 7

JAQUES
All the world's a stage,
And all the men and women merely players.
They have their exits and their entrances,
And one man in his time plays many parts,
His acts being seven ages. At first the infant,
Mewling and puking in the nurse's arms.
Then the whining schoolboy with his satchel
And shining morning face, creeping like snail
Unwillingly to school. And then the lover,
Sighing like furnace, with a woeful ballad
Made to his mistress' eyebrow. Then, a soldier,
Full of strange oaths, and bearded like the pard,
Jealous in honour, sudden, and quick in quarrel,
Seeking the bubble reputation
Even in the cannon's mouth. And then the justice,
In fair round belly with good capon lined,
With eyes severe and beard of formal cut,
Full of wise saws and modern instances;
And so he plays his part. The sixth age shifts
Into the lean and slippered pantaloon,
With spectacles on nose and pouch on side,
His youthful hose, well saved, a world too wide
For his shrunk shank, and his big, manly voice,
Turning again toward childish treble, pipes

And whistles in his sound. Last scene of all,
That ends this strange, eventful history,
Is second childishness and mere oblivion,
Sans teeth, sans eyes, sans taste, sans everything.

# I

## INFANT

—◆—

At first the infant,
Mewling and puking in the nurse's arms.

# Richard III

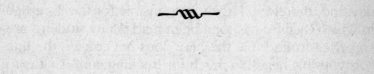

There is no record of when the first performance of *Richard III* was given, but late 1592 or early 1593 is a reasonable assumption. It was a firm favourite in its day and, therefore, largely responsible for the ill-repute in which Richard has long been held. Many students are surprised to find that the play does not contain the line 'Off with his head! So much for Buckingham!' That is to be found in Colley Cibber's adaptation of 1700 in which he himself played the title role.

Richard, Duke of Gloucester and younger brother of Edward IV, is determined to inherit the crown of the dying King. To help him achieve this, he plans the systematic extermination of all those who could possibly hinder his succession.

Although Shakespeare portrays Richard as a villain whose soul is as deformed as his body, the blackness of his character is considerably relieved by his courage, wit and freedom from self-delusion. Included here because he reflects on his birth and his birthright, is a speech from Act 1, Scene 1.

RICHARD

Now is the winter of our discontent
Made glorious summer by this son of York;
And all the clouds that loured upon our house
In the deep bosom of the ocean buried.
Now are our brows bound with victorious wreaths,
Our bruisèd arms hung up for monuments,
Our stern alarums changed to merry meetings,
Our dreadful marches to delightful measures.
Grim-visaged war hath smoothed his wrinkled front,
And now – instead of mounting barbèd steeds
To fright the souls of fearful adversaries—
He capers nimbly in a lady's chamber
To the lascivious pleasing of a lute.
But I, that am not shaped for sportive tricks
Nor made to court an amorous looking-glass,
I that am rudely stamped and want love's majesty
To strut before a wanton ambling nymph,
I that am curtailed of this fair proportion,
Cheated of feature by dissembling nature,
Deformed, unfinished, sent before my time
Into this breathing world scarce half made up—
And that so lamely and unfashionable
That dogs bark at me as I halt by them—
Why, I in this weak piping time of peace
Have no delight to pass away the time,
Unless to spy my shadow in the sun
And descant on mine own deformity.
And therefore since I cannot prove a lover
To entertain these fair well-spoken days,

I am determinèd to prove a villain
And hate the idle pleasures of these days.
Plots have I laid, inductions dangerous,
By drunken prophecies, libels and dreams
To set my brother Clarence and the King
In deadly hate the one against the other.
And if King Edward be as true and just
As I am subtle false and treacherous,
This day should Clarence closely be mewed up
About a prophecy which says that 'G'
Of Edward's heirs the murderer shall be.

# Sonnet 2

Shakespeare composed most of his 154 sonnets in the 1590s. Written in the form of three quatrains and a couplet, the poems had an intriguing dedication: 'To the onlie begetter of these ensuing sonnets. Mr W.H.'.

Some scholars have identified the mysterious 'W.H.' as Henry Wriothesley, Earl of Southampton, to whom Shakespeare had dedicated other works. Others believe him to be William Herbert, Earl of Pembroke, dedicatee of the first folio edition of 1623. Whether he wrote them for himself, his friends or his patrons, Shakespeare's sonnets include some of the finest love poems in the English language.

In the second sonnet, the writer warns that the beauty of one's youth will be worth nothing in old age unless it has been invested wisely.

When forty winters shall besiege thy brow
And dig deep trenches in thy beauty's field,
Thy youth's proud livery, so gazed on now,
Will be a tattered weed, of small worth held.
Then being asked where all thy beauty lies,
Where all the treasure of thy lusty days,
To say within thine own deep-sunken eyes
Were an all-eating shame and thriftless praise.
How much more praise deserved thy beauty's use
If thou couldst answer 'This fair child of mine
Shall sum my count, and make my old excuse',
Proving his beauty by succession thine.
  This were to be new made when thou art old,
    And see thy blood warm when thou feel'st it cold.

# Henry IV, Part 1

In the First Part of *Henry IV*, Shakespeare depicts the early years of the King's reign and, more specifically, the problem caused by the rebellions led by Worcester, Hotspur (Harry Percy) and Owain Glyndŵr.

This was the first of Shakespeare's 'history plays' to make extensive use of comedy, and in the first printing of 1598 there is a reference to 'The humorous conceits of Sir John Falstaff', whom we meet again later in this selection. In the first stage production the character was named Sir John Oldcastle after the Protestant martyr, but eventually the name Falstaff was restored in deference to protests from Oldcastle's descendants.

In this extract from Act 3, Scene 1, Hotspur, eldest son of the powerful Earl of Northumberland, refuses to yield his prisoners to the King unless his kinsman Edmund Mortimer, captured by Owain Glyndŵr, is ransomed.

HOTSPUR

Lord Mortimer and cousin Glyndŵr,
Will you sit down? And uncle Worcester?
    [*Mortimer, Glyndŵr, and Worcester sit*]
A plague upon it, I have forgot the map!

GLYNDŴR

No, here it is. Sit, cousin Percy, sit,
Good cousin Hotspur;
    [*Hotspur sits*]
For by that name
As oft as Lancaster doth speak of you,
His cheek looks pale, and with a rising sigh
He wisheth you in heaven.

HOTSPUR

And you in hell,
As oft as he hears Owain Glyndŵr spoke of.

GLYNDŴR

I cannot blame him. At my nativity
The front of heaven was full of fiery shapes,
Of burning cressets; and at my birth
The frame and huge foundation of the earth
Shaked like a coward.

HOTSPUR

Why, so it would have done
At the same season if your mother's cat
Had but kittened, though yourself had never been
    born.

GLYNDŴR

I say the earth did shake when I was born.

19

HOTSPUR

And I say the earth was not of my mind
If you suppose as fearing you it shook.

GLYNDŴR

The heavens were all on fire, the earth did tremble–

HOTSPUR

O, then the earth shook to see the heavens on fire,
And not in fear of your nativity.
Diseased nature oftentimes breaks forth
In strange eruptions; oft the teeming earth
Is with a kind of colic pinched and vexed
By the imprisoning of unruly wind
Within her womb, which for enlargement striving
Shakes the old beldam earth, and topples down
Steeples and moss-grown towers. At your birth
Our grandam earth, having this distemp'rature,
In passion shook.

GLYNDŴR

Cousin, of many men
I do not bear these crossings. Give me leave
To tell you once again that at my birth
The front of heaven was full of fiery shapes,
The goats ran from the mountains, and the herds
Were strangely clamorous to the frighted fields.
These signs have marked me extraordinary,
And all the courses of my life do show
I am not in the roll of commen men.
Where is he living, clipped in with the sea
That chides the banks of England, Scotland, Wales,
Which calls me pupil or hath read to me?

And bring him out that is but woman's son
Can trace me in the tedious ways of art,
And hold me pace in deep experiments.
HOTSPUR
[*standing*]
I think there's no man speaketh better Welsh.
I'll to dinner.
MORTIMER
Peace, cousin Percy, you will make him mad.
GLYNDŴR
I can call spirits from the vasty deep.
HOTSPUR
Why, so can I, or so can any man;
But will they come when you do call for them?
GLYNDŴR
Why, I can teach you, cousin, to command the
devil.
HOTSPUR
And I can teach thee, coz, to shame the devil,
By telling truth: 'Tell truth, and shame the devil'.
If thou have power to raise him, bring him hither,
And I'll be sworn I have power to shame him hence.
O, while you live, tell truth and shame the devil.
MORTIMER
Come, come, no more of this unprofitable chat.
GLYNDŴR
Three times hath Henry Bolingbroke made head
Against my power; thrice from the banks of Wye
And sandy-bottomed Severn have I sent him
Bootless home, and weather-beaten back.

21

HOTSPUR

   Home without boots, and in foul weather too!

   How scapes he agues, in the devil's name?

GLYNDŴR

   Come, here's the map. Shall we divide our right,

   According to our threefold order ta'en?

MORTIMER

   The Archdeacon hath divided it

   Into three limits very equally.

   England from Trent and Severn hitherto

   By south and east is to my part assigned;

   All westward – Wales beyond the Severn shore

   And all the fertile land within that bound–

   To Owain Glyndŵr; [*to Hotspur*] and, dear coz, to you

   The remnant northward lying off from Trent.

   And our indentures tripartite are drawn,

   Which, being sealèd interchangeably–

   A business that this night may execute–

   Tomorrow, cousin Percy, you and I

   And my good lord of Worcester will set forth

   To meet your father and the Scottish power,

   As is appointed us, at Shrewsbury.

   My father, Glyndŵr, is not ready yet,

   Nor shall we need his help these fourteen days.

   Within that space you may have drawn together

   Your tenants, friends, and neighbouring gentlemen.

GLYNDŴR

   A shorter time shall send me to you, lords;

And in my conduct shall your ladies come,
From whom you now must steal and take no leave;
For there will be a world of water shed
Upon the parting of your wives and you.

# King Lear

In Shakespeare's day, *The History of King Lear* was not the most popular of his plays, the tragic elements possibly being unacceptable to his pleasure-loving Elizabethan audiences. The playwright Nahum Tate (1652–1715) capitalised on this by giving his adaptation a happy ending, and it was this version that held the stage from 1681–1843.

King Lear was the central figure in the *History of the Kings of Britain* by Geoffrey of Monmouth. For his tragedy, however, Shakespeare probably used the version of the Lear story found in Holinshed's *Chronicles* – a book he was already familiar with, from his search for suitable plots.

There is one further possibility for the original source of the plot. In 1603, Lady Wildgoose and her sister Lady Sandys tried to get their aged father, Brian Annesley, registered as insane. Their endeavours were frustrated by their sister Cordell. Perhaps Shakespeare heard gossip about it!

At the start of the play, Shakespeare asks us to focus on the relationship between a doting – if irascible – father and his children. By Act 1, Scene 4, when he finds his daughters' sentiments to have been insincere and based on greed and acquisition, Lear's own love turns to a cruel and bitter hatred.

LEAR

Darkness and devils!
Saddle my horses, call my train together!–
      [*Exit one or more*]
Degenerate bastard, I'll not trouble thee.
Yet have I left a daughter.

GONERIL

You strike my people, and your disordered rabble
Make servants of their betters.
      *Enter the Duke of Albany*

LEAR

Woe, that too late repent's – O sir, are you come?
Is it your will that we – prepare my horses.
      [*Exit one or more*]
Ingratitude, thou marble-hearted fiend,
More hideous when thou show'st thee in a child
Than the sea-monster – [*to Goneril*] detested kite,
   thou liest.
My train are men of choice and rarest parts,
That all particulars of duty know,
And in the most exact regard support
The worships of their name. O most small fault,
How ugly didst thou in Cordelia show,
That, like an engine, wrenched my frame of nature
From the fixed place, drew from my heart all love,
And added to the gall! O Lear, Lear!
Beat at this gate that let thy folly in
And thy dear judgement out. – Go, go, my people!

ALBANY

My lord, I am guiltless as I am ignorant.

LEAR
It may be so, my lord. Hark, nature, hear:
Dear goddess, suspend thy purpose if
Thou didst intend to make this creature fruitful.
Into her womb convey sterility.
Dry up in her the organs of increase,
And from her derogate body never spring
A babe to honour her. If she must teem,
Create her child of spleen, that it may live
And be a thwart disnatured torment to her.
Let it stamp wrinkles in her brow of youth,
With cadent tears fret channels in her cheeks,
Turn all her mother's pains and benefits
To laughter and contempt, that she may feel–
That she may feel
How sharper than a serpent's tooth it is
To have a thankless child. – Go, go, my people!

# II
## SCHOOLBOY

—⚬—

And then the whining schoolboy, with his satchel
And shining morning face, creeping like snail
Unwillingly to school.

# Hamlet

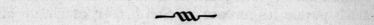

Although *Hamlet* is a play of revenge, its unique place in world literature owes much to the thoughtful and philosophical nature of its principal character. He does not so much pursue his revenge, as find himself caught up in events that lead him to murder his own family. His feigned madness, melancholy and introspection often make his behaviour seem more childlike than that of most children.

In this play, more than any other, Shakespeare reveals his profound insight into human nature – equalled, perhaps, only by Sigmund Freud who may well have associated Hamlet's behaviour with a male child's overweening adoration of his mother.

'In point of fact, there is no such thing as Shakespeare's Hamlet. If Hamlet has something of the definiteness of a work of art, he has also all the obscurity that belongs to life. There are as many Hamlets as there are melancholies.' Oscar Wilde, *The Critic As Artist*

*Hamlet* is one of the longest of Shakespeare's plays – a minimum of three and a half hours. This did not daunt a young actor in Huddersfield who regarded the title role as his 'big break'. Unfortunately, his costume did not match his aspirations. Dressed in a ridiculously small pair of tights, he had the audience laughing quietly to themselves at his very first entrance. But when he delivered the last two lines of only his fourth speech in the play:

'But I have that within which passeth show–
These but the trappings and the suits of woe'

he brought the house down.

The novelist Anthony Burgess once discovered a film version of *Hamlet* in Hindi, which included a dance of grave-diggers and ten songs for Ophelia. It also had English subtitles, one of which was: 'Shall I live or do myself in? I do not know . . .'

Even though Shakespeare was a resident playwright with his own theatre and troupe of actors, there was no effective dramatic copyright to protect his work. Consequently, there were many unauthorised versions, or 'bad' quartos as they came to be known. This was not necessarily due to the quality of the printing, but because the texts had been put together from memory by actors and even, on occasion, by spectators.

By way of introduction to Hamlet's most famous soliloquy as written by Shakespeare himself, here is how it appeared in the 'bad' quarto of 1603.

*To be, or not to be, I there's the point,*

*To Die, to fleepe, is that all? I all:*
*No, to fleepe, to dreame, I mary there it goes,*
*For in that dreame of death, when wee awake,*
*And borne before an euerlafting ludge,*
*From whence no paffenger euer retur'nd,*
*Thee vndifcouered country, at whofe fight*
*The happy fmile, and the accurfed damn'd.*
*But for this, the ioyfull hope of this,*
*Whol'd beare the fcornes and flattery of the world,*
*Scorned by the right rich, the rich curffed of the poore?*

*The widow being oppreffed, the orphan wrong'd,*
*The tafte of hunger, or a tirants raigne,*
*And thoufand more calamities befides,*
*To grunt and fweate vnder this weary life,*
*When that he may his full Quietus make,*
*With a bare bodkin, who would this indure,*
*But for a hope of fomething after death?*
*Which pufles the braine, and doth confound the fence,*
*Which makes vs rather beare thofe euilles we haue,*
*Than flie to others that we know not of.*
*I that, O this confcience makes cowardes of vs all,*
*Lady in thy orizons, be all my finnes remembred.*

## *Act 3, Scene 1*

At this moment in the play, Hamlet's father's ghost has appeared to his son demanding revenge for his murder. The young Prince, however, is beset by doubts and remains indecisive.

HAMLET

    To be, or not to be; that is the question:
    Whether 'tis nobler in the mind to suffer
    The slings and arrows of outrageous fortune,
    Or to take arms against a sea of troubles,
    And, by opposing, end them. To die, to sleep–
    No more, and by a sleep to say we end
    The heartache and the thousand natural shocks
    That flesh is heir to – 'tis a consummation
    Devoutly to be wished. To die, to sleep.
    To sleep, perchance to dream. Ay, there's the rub,
    For in that sleep of death what dreams may come
    When we have shuffled off this mortal coil
    Must give us pause. There's the respect
    That makes calamity of so long life,
    For who would bear the whips and scorns of time,
    Th'oppressor's wrong, the proud man's contumely,
    The pangs of disprized love, the law's delay,
    The insolence of office, and the spurns
    That patient merit of th'unworthy takes,
    When he himself might his quietus make

With a bare bodkin? Who would these fardels bear,
To grunt and sweat under a weary life,
But that the dread of something after death,
The undiscovered country from whose bourn
No traveller returns, puzzles the will,
And makes us rather bear those ills we have
Than fly to others that we know not of?
Thus conscience does make cowards of us all,
And thus the native hue of resolution
Is sicklied o'er with the pale cast of thought,
And enterprises of great pith and moment
With this regard their currents turn awry,
And lose the name of action. . . .

# Coriolanus

*Coriolanus* is Shakespeare's last Roman play, following on from *Julius Caesar* and *Antony and Cleopatra*. Written in 1608, its direct source was Thomas North's translation (1579) of Plutarch's *Lives* which gives an account of the legendary patrician Coriolanus. Shakespeare would have relied on this work for information on the corn riots of Ancient Rome although similar occurrences in England during 1607 and 1608 may well have stimulated his interest in the story.

Set in the fifth century BC when Rome was an aristo-cratically controlled republic, *Coriolanus* examines the relationship between personal ambition and national destiny. Although the central character is both arrogant and selfish, he is, nevertheless, a man of integrity who finally yields to the tenderness that will lead to his destruction.

In Act 5, Scene 3, we see a mother and son locked in the sort of bitter disagreement that all too often occurs between parents and their children. Enraged by the way he has been treated by the Plebeians, Coriolanus joins forces with the Volscians – traditional enemies of Rome – and is about to launch an attack on the city.

CORIOLANUS

What's this?

Your knees to me? To your corrected son?
  [*He raises her*]
Then let the pebbles on the hungry beach
Fillip the stars; then let the mutinous winds
Strike the proud cedars 'gainst the fiery sun,
Murd'ring impossibility to make
What cannot be slight work.

VOLUMNIA

Thou art my warrior.
I holp to frame thee. Do you know this lady?

CORIOLANUS

The noble sister of Publicola,
The moon of Rome, chaste as the icicle
That's candied by the frost from purest snow
And hangs on Dian's temple – dear Valeria!

VOLUMNIA

[*showing Coriolanus his son*]
This is a poor epitome of yours,
Which by th' interpretation of full time
May show like all yourself.

CORIOLANUS

[*to Young Martius*]
The god of soldiers,
With the consent of supreme Jove, inform
Thy thoughts with nobleness, that thou mayst prove
To shame unvulnerable, and stick i'th' wars
Like a great sea-mark standing every flaw
And saving those that eye thee!

VOLUMNIA
[*to Young Martius*]
Your knee, sirrah.
[*Young Martius kneels*]

CORIOLANUS
That's my brave boy.

VOLUMNIA
Even he, your wife, this lady, and myself
Are suitors to you.

CORIOLANUS
I beseech you, peace.
Or if you'd ask, remember this before:
The things I have forsworn to grant may never
Be held by you denials. Do not bid me
Dismiss my soldiers, or capitulate
Again with Rome's mechanics. Tell me not
Wherein I seem unnatural. Desire not t'allay
My rages and revenges with your colder reasons.

VOLUMNIA
O, no more, no more!
You have said you will not grant us anything–
For we have nothing else to ask but that
Which you deny already. Yet we will ask,
That, if you fail in our request, the blame
May hang upon your hardness. Therefore hear us.

CORIOLANUS
Aufidius and you Volsces, mark, for we'll
Hear naught from Rome in private.
[*He sits*]
Your request?

VOLUMNIA
Should we be silent and not speak, our raiment
And state of bodies would bewray what life
We have led since thy exile. Think with thyself
How more unfortunate than all living women
Are we come hither, since that thy sight, which should
Make our eyes flow with joy, hearts dance with
    comforts,
Constrains them weep and shake with fear and sor-
    row,
Making the mother, wife, and child to see
The son, the husband, and the father tearing
His country's bowels out; and to poor we
Thine enmity's most capital. Thou barr'st us
Our prayers to the gods, which is a comfort
That all but we enjoy. For how can we,
Alas, how can we for our country pray,
Whereto we are bound, together with thy victory,
Whereto we are bound? Alack, or we must lose
The country, our dear nurse, or else thy person,
Our comfort in the country. We must find
An evident calamity, though we had
Our wish which side should win. For either thou
Must as a foreign recreant be led
With manacles thorough our streets, or else
Triumphantly tread on thy country's ruin,
And bear the palm for having bravely shed
Thy wife and children's blood. For myself, son,
I purpose not to wait on fortune till
These wars determine. If I cannot persuade thee

Rather to show a noble grace to both parts
Than seek the end of one, thou shalt no sooner
March to assault thy country than to tread–
Trust to't, thou shalt not – on thy mother's womb
That brought thee to this world.

# Macbeth

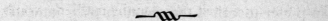

Although Shakespeare's shortest play, *Macbeth* is one of his best known and loved – despite the notorious superstitions that surround it: so much so, that actors prefer to call it the 'Scottish play' rather than risk the bad luck associated with using its proper title.

Theatre people are never short of stories to back up their belief that *Macbeth* can bring bad luck. An actor at Oldham Rep was actually killed onstage during a performance of the play; at Greenwich, a member of the cast fell off a rostrum and was in hospital for months; at Salisbury the stage manager inadvertently mentioned the title and at that moment part of the scenery collapsed onstage. And this catalogue of disasters would hardly be complete without mentioning Peter O'Toole's bloodstained fiasco which ran for only a few nights at the Old Vic in the 1980s.

The three witches whose prophecies start Macbeth on his tragic and ambitious course are probably the most famous in literature. For much of the plot, Shakespeare used the account of the reigns of the Scottish kings Duncan and Macbeth in Holinshed's *Chronicles of England, Scotland and Ireland* (1578). The addition of the witches, however, is Shakespeare's own invention, and he created a far more evil and introspective leading character than the uncomplicated warrior king portrayed by Holinshed.

Childbirth and infancy are recurring themes in the play and, in the scene that follows, the witches refer to 'finger of birth-strangled babe' – one of the ingredients for a magic brew they are preparing that will allow Macbeth to consult the apparitions.

## Act 4, Scene 1

FIRST WITCH

Thrice the brinded cat hath mewed.

SECOND WITCH

Thrice, and once the hedge-pig whined.

THIRD WITCH

Harpier cries ''Tis time, 'tis time.'

FIRST WITCH

Round about the cauldron go,
In the poisoned entrails throw.
Toad that under cold stone
Days and nights has thirty-one
Sweltered venom sleeping got,
Boil thou first i'th' charmèd pot.

ALL

Double, double, toil and trouble,
Fire burn, and cauldron bubble.

SECOND WITCH

Fillet of a fenny snake,
In the cauldron boil and bake.
Eye of newt and toe of frog,
Wool of bat and tongue of dog,
Adder's fork and blind-worm's sting,
Lizard's leg and owlet's wing,

For a charm of powerful trouble,
Like a hell-broth broil and bubble.

ALL

Double, double, toil and trouble,
Fire burn, and cauldron bubble.

THIRD WITCH

Scale of dragon, tooth of wolf,
Witches' mummy, maw and gulf
Of the ravined salt-sea shark,
Root of hemlock digged i'th' dark,
Liver of blaspheming Jew,
Gall of goat, and slips of yew
Slivered in the moon's eclipse,
Nose of Turk, and Tartar's lips,
Finger of birth-strangled babe
Ditch-delivered by a drab,
Make the gruel thick and slab.
Add thereto a tiger's chaudron
For th'ingredience of our cauldron.

ALL

Double, double, toil and trouble,
Fire burn, and cauldron bubble.

SECOND WITCH

Cool it with a baboon's blood,
Then the charm is firm and good.
    [*Enter Hecate and the other three Witches*]

HECATE

O, well done! I commend your pains,
And everyone shall share i'th' gains.
And now about the cauldron sing

Like elves and fairies in a ring,
Enchanting all that you put in.
    [*Music and a song*]
Black spirits and white, red spirits and grey,
Mingle, mingle, mingle, you that mingle may.

FOURTH WITCH

Titty, Tiffin, keep it stiff in;
Firedrake, Puckey, make it lucky;
Liard, Robin, you must bob in.

ALL

Round, around, around, about, about,
All ill come running in, all good keep out.

FOURTH WITCH

Here's the blood of a bat.

HECATE

Put in that, O put in that!

FIFTH WITCH

Here's leopard's bane.

HECATE

Put in a grain.

FOURTH WITCH

The juice of toad, the oil of adder.

FIFTH WITCH

Those will make the younker madder.

HECATE

Put in, there's all, and rid the stench.

A WITCH

Nay, here's three ounces of a red-haired wench.

ALL

Round, around, around, about, about,

All ill come running in, all good keep out.

SECOND WITCH

By the pricking of my thumbs,
Something wicked this way comes.

# III

## LOVER

—⚭—

And then the lover,
Sighing like furnace, with a woeful ballad
Made to his mistress' eyebrow.

# Sonnet 18

Shakespeare's sonnets fall into two main groups. Nos. 1–126 are addressed to a beloved friend; nos. 127–152 to a woman, the fascinating 'dark lady' whom the poet loves in spite of himself and her unworthiness. The last two sonnets, 153 and 154, belong to neither category and were possibly early poetic exercises.

In Sonnet 18, the writer declares that even nature herself is eclipsed by the beauty of his loved one.

Shall I compare thee to a summer's day?
Thou art more lovely and more temperate.
Rough winds do shake the darling buds of May,
And summer's lease hath all too short a date.
Sometime too hot the eye of heaven shines,
And often is his gold complexion dimmed,
And every fair from fair sometime declines,
By chance or nature's changing course untrimmed;
But thy eternal summer shall not fade
Nor lose possession of that fair thou ow'st,
Nor shall death brag thou wander'st in his shade
When in eternal lines to time thou grow'st.
　　So long as men can breathe or eyes can see,
　　So long lives this, and this gives life to thee.

# Romeo and Juliet

Shakespeare's lovers are among the best known in literature: Antony and Cleopatra, Beatrice and Benedick, Othello, Desdemona, Orlando, Rosalind, and many more.

The most celebrated of them all, Romeo and Juliet, first appeared in the *Novellino* of Masuccio Salernitano in 1476, although Shakespeare based his drama mainly on the retelling of that story in *The Tragical History of Romeus and Juliet* by Arthur Brooke (1562).

On its first appearance in print in 1597, the play was described as 'an excellent conceited tragedie as it hath been often (with great applause) plaid publiquely'. Since then, there have been many film and ballet versions of the story, and it has inspired musical scores by Tchaikovsky and Prokofiev as well as Leonard Bernstein's *West Side Story*.

Our first extract takes place not long after Romeo has met Juliet for the first time at a great ball given by her parents. Despite the deadly feud that exists between their families, the Montagues and the Capulets, Romeo risks death to see Juliet once more.

## Act 2, Scene 1

ROMEO
[*coming forward*]
He jests at scars that never felt a wound.
But soft, what light through yonder window breaks?
It is the east, and Juliet is the sun.
Arise, fair sun, and kill the envious moon,
Who is already sick and pale with grief
That thou, her maid, art far more fair than she.
Be not her maid, since she is envious.
Her vestal livery is but sick and green,
And none but fools do wear it; cast it off.
    [*Enter Juliet aloft*]
It is my lady, O, it is my love.
O that she knew she were!
She speaks, yet she says nothing. What of that?
Her eye discourses; I will answer it.
I am too bold. 'Tis not to me she speaks.
Two of the fairest stars in all the heaven,
Having some business, do entreat her eyes
To twinkle in their spheres till they return.
What if her eyes were there, they in her head?–
The brightness of her cheek would shame those stars
As daylight doth a lamp; her eye in heaven
Would through the airy region stream so bright
That birds would sing and think it were not night.
See how she leans her cheek upon her hand.

O, that I were a glove upon that hand,
That I might touch that cheek!

JULIET

Ay me.

ROMEO

[*aside*]

She speaks.
O, speak again, bright angel; for thou art
As glorious to this night, being o'er my head,
As is a wingèd messenger of heaven
Unto the white upturnèd wond'ring eyes
Of mortals that fall back to gaze on him
When he bestrides the lazy-passing clouds
And sails upon the bosom of the air.

JULIET

[*not knowing Romeo hears her*]

O Romeo, Romeo, wherefore art thou Romeo?
Deny thy father and refuse thy name,
Or if thou wilt not, be but sworn my love,
And I'll no longer be a Capulet.

ROMEO

[*aside*]

Shall I hear more, or shall I speak at this?

JULIET

'Tis but thy name that is my enemy.
Thou art thyself, though not a Montague.
What's Montague? It is nor hand, nor foot,
Nor arm, nor face, nor any other part
Belonging to a man. O, be some other name!
What's in a name? That which we call a rose

By any other word would smell as sweet.
So Romeo would, were he not Romeo called,
Retain that dear perfection which he owes
Without that title. Romeo, doff thy name,
And for thy name – which is no part of thee–
Take all myself.

ROMEO

[*to Juliet*]
I take thee at thy word.
Call me but love and I'll be new baptized.
Henceforth I never will be Romeo.

JULIET

What man art thou that, thus bescreened in night,
So stumblest on my counsel?

ROMEO

By a name
I know not how to tell thee who I am.
My name, dear saint, is hateful to myself
Because it is an enemy to thee.
Had I it written, I would tear the word.

JULIET

My ears have yet not drunk a hundred words
Of thy tongue's uttering, yet I know the sound.
Art thou not Romeo, and a Montague?

ROMEO

Neither, fair maid, if either thee dislike.

JULIET

How cam'st thou hither, tell me, and wherefore?
The orchard walls are high and hard to climb,
And the place death, considering who thou art,

If any of my kinsmen find thee here.

ROMEO

With love's light wings did I o'erperch these walls,
For stony limits cannot hold love out,
And what love can do, that dares love attempt.
Therefore thy kinsmen are no stop to me.

JULIET

If they do see thee, they will murder thee.

ROMEO

Alack, there lies more peril in thine eye
Than twenty of their swords. Look thou but sweet,
And I am proof against their enmity.

# The Taming of the Shrew

There have been many adaptations of this robust comedy over the centuries, and Shakespeare himself may have 'borrowed' the work from *The Taming of a Shrew* – a play that appeared in print as early as 1594. Some scholars have even suggested that he wrote both versions, but the generally accepted view is that Shakespeare's play was written first and that an anonymous imitation was written later in the hope of capitalising on its success.

Neither of the two principal characters – Petruccio, a gentleman of Verona, and Katherine, the 'shrew' – is cast from the mould of classic lovers. Nevertheless, their conflict has been used to great effect by other writers ever since the play first appeared in the 1623 Folio.

Many of us first got to know the story through that wonderful Cole Porter musical *Kiss Me Kate* which taught those who did not know it already that Shakespeare could actually be fun!

Katherine is a maiden of such a violent temper that it seems unlikely she will ever find a husband. In Act 2, Scene 1, she meets Petruccio for the first time, hardly suspecting him to be the man she will eventually marry.

PETRUCCIO
  Good morrow, Kate, for that's your name, I hear.
KATHERINE
  Well have you heard, but something hard of hearing.
  They call me Katherine that do talk of me.
PETRUCCIO
  You lie, in faith, for you are called plain Kate,
  And bonny Kate, and sometimes Kate the curst,
  But Kate, the prettiest Kate in Christendom,
  Kate of Kate Hall, my super-dainty Kate–
  For dainties are all cates, and therefore 'Kate'–
  Take this of me, Kate of my consolation:
  Hearing thy mildness praised in every town,
  Thy virtues spoke of, and thy beauty sounded–
  Yet not so deeply as to thee belongs–
  Myself am moved to woo thee for my wife.
KATHERINE
  Moved? In good time. Let him that moved you hither
  Re-move you hence. I knew you at the first
  You were a movable.
PETRUCCIO
  Why, what's a movable?
KATHERINE
  A joint-stool.
PETRUCCIO
  Thou hast hit it. Come, sit on me.
KATHERINE
  Asses are made to bear, and so are you.
PETRUCCIO
  Women are made to bear, and so are you.

KATHERINE

No such jade as you, if me you mean.

PETRUCCIO

Alas, good Kate, I will not burden thee,
For knowing thee to be but young and light.

KATHERINE

Too light for such a swain as you to catch,
And yet as heavy as my weight should be.

PETRUCCIO

Should be? – should buzz.

KATHERINE

Well ta'en, and like a buzzard.

PETRUCCIO

O slow-winged turtle, shall a buzzard take thee?

KATHERINE

Ay, for a turtle, as he takes a buzzard.

PETRUCCIO

Come, come, you wasp, i'faith you are too angry.

KATHERINE

If I be waspish, best beware my sting.

PETRUCCIO

My remedy is then to pluck it out.

KATHERINE

Ay, if the fool could find it where it lies.

PETRUCCIO

Who knows not where a wasp does wear his sting?
In his tail.

KATHERINE

In his tongue.

PETRUCCIO
   Whose tongue?
KATHERINE
   Yours, if you talk of tales, and so farewell.
PETRUCCIO
   What, with my tongue in your tail? Nay, come again,
   Good Kate, I am a gentleman.
KATHERINE
   That I'll try.
       [*She strikes him*]
PETRUCCIO
   I swear I'll cuff you if you strike again.
KATHERINE
   So may you lose your arms.
   If you strike me you are no gentleman,
   And if no gentleman, why then, no arms.
PETRUCCIO
   A herald, Kate? O, put me in thy books.
KATHERINE
   What is your crest – a coxcomb?
PETRUCCIO
   A combless cock, so Kate will be my hen.
KATHERINE
   No cock of mine. You crow too like a craven.
PETRUCCIO
   Nay, come, Kate, come. You must not look so sour.
KATHERINE
   It is my fashion when I see a crab.
PETRUCCIO
   Why, here's no crab, and therefore look not sour.

KATHERINE
There is, there is.

PETRUCCIO
Then show it me.

KATHERINE
Had I a glass I would.

PETRUCCIO
What, you mean my face?

KATHERINE
Well aimed, of such a young one.

PETRUCCIO
Now, by Saint George, I am too young for you.

KATHERINE
Yet you are withered.

PETRUCCIO
'Tis with cares.

KATHERINE
I care not.

PETRUCCIO
Nay, hear you, Kate. In sooth, you scape not so.

KATHERINE
I chafe you if I tarry. Let me go.

PETRUCCIO
No, not a whit. I find you passing gentle.
'Twas told me you were rough, and coy, and sullen,
And now I find report a very liar,
For thou art pleasant, gamesome, passing courteous,
But slow in speech, yet sweet as springtime flowers.
Thou canst not frown. Thou canst not look askance,
Nor bite the lip, as angry wenches will,

Nor hast thou pleasure to be cross in talk,
But thou with mildness entertain'st thy wooers,
With gentle conference, soft, and affable.
Why does the world report that Kate doth limp?
O sland'rous world! Kate like the hazel twig
Is straight and slender, and as brown in hue
As hazelnuts, and sweeter than the kernels.
O let me see thee walk. Thou dost not halt.

KATHERINE
Go, fool, and whom thou keep'st command.

PETRUCCIO
Did ever Dian so become a grove
As Kate this chamber with her princely gait?
O, be thou Dian, and let her be Kate,
And then let Kate be chaste and Dian sportful.

KATHERINE
Where did you study all this goodly speech?

PETRUCCIO
It is extempore, from my mother-wit.

KATHERINE
A witty mother, witless else her son.

PETRUCCIO
Am I not wise?

KATHERINE
Yes, keep you warm.

PETRUCCIO
Marry, so I mean, sweet Katherine, in thy bed.
And therefore setting all this chat aside,
Thus in plain terms: your father hath consented
That you shall be my wife, your dowry 'greed on,

And will you, nill you, I will marry you.
Now, Kate, I am a husband for your turn,
For by this light, whereby I see thy beauty–
Thy beauty that doth make me like thee well–
Thou must be married to no man but me,

*Enter Baptista, Gremio and Tranio as Lucentio*

For I am he am born to tame you, Kate,
And bring you from a wild Kate to a Kate
Conformable as other household Kates.
Here comes your father. Never make denial.
I must and will have Katherine to my wife.

BAPTISTA

Now, Signor Petruccio, how speed you with my
daughter?

PETRUCCIO

How but well, sir, how but well?
It were impossible I should speed amiss.

BAPTISTA

Why, how now, daughter Katherine – in your dumps?

KATHERINE

Call you me daughter? Now I promise you
You have showed a tender fatherly regard,
To wish me wed to one half-lunatic,
A madcap ruffian and a swearing Jack,
That thinks with oaths to face the matter out.

PETRUCCIO

Father, 'tis thus: yourself and all the world
That talked of her have talked amiss of her.
If she be curst, it is for policy,
For she's not froward, but modest as the dove.

She is not hot, but temperate as the morn.
For patience she will prove a second Grissel,
And Roman Lucrece for her chastity.
And to conclude, we have 'greed so well together
That upon Sunday is the wedding day.

KATHERINE
I'll see thee hanged on Sunday first.

GREMIO
Hark, Petruccio, she says she'll see thee hanged first.

TRANIO
Is this your speeding? Nay then, goodnight our part.

PETRUCCIO
Be patient, gentlemen. I choose her for myself.
If she and I be pleased, what's that to you?
'Tis bargained 'twixt us twain, being alone,
That she shall still be curst in company.
I tell you, 'tis incredible to believe
How much she loves me. O, the kindest Kate!
She hung about my neck, and kiss on kiss
She vied so fast, protesting oath on oath,
That in a twink she won me to her love.
O, you are novices. 'Tis a world to see
How tame, when men and women are alone,
A meacock wretch can make the curstest shrew.
Give me thy hand, Kate. I will unto Venice,
To buy apparel 'gainst the wedding day.
Provide the feast, father, and bid the guests.
I will be sure my Katherine shall be fine.

BAPTISTA
I know not what to say, but give me your hands.

God send you joy, Petruccio! 'Tis a match.

**GREMIO** *and* **TRANIO**

Amen, say we. We will be witnesses.

**PETRUCCIO**

Father, and wife, and gentlemen, adieu.
I will to Venice. Sunday comes apace.
We will have rings, and things, and fine array;
And kiss me, Kate. We will be married o' Sunday.

# Sonnet 57

In Sonnet 57, the poet describes some of the bitter-sweet feelings that those in love have to bear even when they know them to be foolish.


Being your slave, what should I do but tend
Upon the hours and times of your desire?
I have no precious time at all to spend,
Nor services to do, till you require;
Nor dare I chide the world-without-end hour
Whilst I, my sovereign, watch the clock for you,
Nor think the bitterness of absence sour
When you have bid your servant once adieu.
Nor dare I question with my jealous thought
Where you may be, or your affairs suppose,
But like a sad slave stay and think of naught
Save, where you are, how happy you make those.
    So true a fool is love that in your will,
    Though you do anything, he thinks no ill.

# Richard III

—❦—

What many regarded as the best-ever portrayal of Richard was given by John Barrymore in 1920. Regrettably, the actor playing Ratcliffe in the same production was not his equal, especially on one disastrous occasion when he should have said:

> 'My lord, 'tis I. The early village cock
> Hath twice done salutation to the morn.'

The unfortunate actor got as far as 'The early village cock . . .' and dried. He tried again: ''Tis I . . . the early village cock . . .' He may well have made a third attempt had Barrymore not hissed, 'Why don't you crow, then?'

Our second visit to the play finds Richard as a would-be lover, despite already having described himself as 'not made to court an amorous looking-glass'.

In a scene which takes place in sight of her father-in-law's coffin, Lady Anne finds Richard's advances totally abhorrent. Despite this – and the fact that he has already killed two members of her family – Richard continues to press his suit.

## Act 1, Scene 2

**LADY ANNE**
  Villain, thou know'st no law of God nor man.
  No beast so fierce but knows some touch of pity.

**RICHARD**
  But I know none, and therefore am no beast.

**LADY ANNE**
  O wonderful, when devils tell the truth!

**RICHARD**
  More wonderful, when angels are so angry.
  Vouchsafe, divine perfection of a woman,
  Of these supposèd crimes to give me leave
  By circumstance but to acquit myself.

**LADY ANNE**
  Vouchsafe, diffused infection of a man,
  Of these known evils but to give me leave
  By circumstance t'accuse thy cursèd self.

**RICHARD**
  Fairer than tongue can name thee, let me have
  Some patient leisure to excuse myself.

**LADY ANNE**
  Fouler than heart can think thee, thou canst make
  No excuse current but to hang thyself.

**RICHARD**
  By such despair I should accuse myself.

**LADY ANNE**
  And by despairing shalt thou stand excused,

For doing worthy vengeance on thyself
That didst unworthy slaughter upon others.

RICHARD

Say that I slew them not.

LADY ANNE

Then say they were not slain.
But dead they are – and, devilish slave, by thee.

RICHARD

I did not kill your husband.

LADY ANNE

Why, then he is alive.

RICHARD

Nay, he is dead, and slain by Edward's hand.

LADY ANNE

In thy foul throat thou liest. Queen Margaret saw
Thy murd'rous falchion smoking in his blood,
The which thou once didst bend against her breast,
But that thy brothers beat aside the point.

RICHARD

I was provokèd by her sland'rous tongue,
That laid their guilt upon my guiltless shoulders.

LADY ANNE

Thou wast provokèd by thy bloody mind,
That never dream'st on aught but butcheries.
Didst thou not kill this king?

RICHARD

I grant ye.

LADY ANNE

Dost grant me, hedgehog? Then God grant me, too,
Thou mayst be damnèd for that wicked deed.

O he was gentle, mild, and virtuous.

RICHARD
The better for the King of Heaven that hath him.

LADY ANNE
He *is* in heaven, where thou shalt never come.

RICHARD
Let him thank me that holp to send him thither,
For he was fitter for that place than earth.

LADY ANNE
And thou unfit for any place but hell.

RICHARD
Yes, one place else, if you will hear my name it.

LADY ANNE
Some dungeon.

RICHARD
Your bedchamber.

LADY ANNE
Ill rest betide the chamber where thou liest.

RICHARD
So will it, madam, till I lie with you.

LADY ANNE
I hope so.

RICHARD
I know so. But gentle Lady Anne,
To leave this keen encounter of our wits
And fall something into a slower method,
Is not the causer of the timeless deaths
Of these Plantagenets, Henry and Edward,
As blameful as the executioner?

LADY ANNE
 Thou wast the cause of that accursed effect.
RICHARD
 Your beauty was the cause of that effect–
 Your beauty that did haunt me in my sleep
 To undertake the death of all the world
 So I might live one hour in your sweet bosom.
LADY ANNE
 If I thought that, I tell thee, homicide,
 These nails should rend that beauty from my cheeks.
RICHARD
 These eyes could not endure sweet beauty's wreck.
 You should not blemish it if I stood by.
 As all the world is cheerèd by the sun,
 So I by that: it is my day, my life.
LADY ANNE
 Black night o'ershade thy day, and death thy life.
RICHARD
 Curse not thyself, fair creature: thou art both.
LADY ANNE
 I would I were, to be revenged on thee.
RICHARD
 It is a quarrel most unnatural,
 To be revenged on him that loveth you.
LADY ANNE
 It is a quarrel just and reasonable,
 To be revenged on him that killed my husband.
RICHARD
 He that bereft thee, lady, of thy husband,
 Did it to help thee to a better husband.

LADY ANNE
  His better doth not breathe upon the earth.
RICHARD
  He lives that loves thee better than he could.
LADY ANNE
  Name him.
RICHARD
  Plantagenet.
LADY ANNE
  Why, that was he.
RICHARD
  The selfsame name, but one of better nature.
LADY ANNE
  Where is he?
RICHARD
  Here.
      [*She spits at him*]
  Why dost thou spit at me?
LADY ANNE
  Would it were mortal poison for thy sake.
RICHARD
  Never came poison from so sweet a place.
LADY ANNE
  Never hung poison on a fouler toad.
  Out of my sight! Thou dost infect mine eyes.
RICHARD
  Thine eyes, sweet lady, have infected mine.

# As You Like It

—m—

There is every possibility that Shakespeare considered the setting for *As You Like It* as being the Ardennes region of France and not the Forest of Arden as popularly supposed. It was certainly in France that Thomas Lodge set his prose romance *Rosalynde* on which Shakespeare based his work.

Whatever the original intention, however, since the late nineteenth century the play has often been performed in an authentic open-air setting.

In this second excerpt, Orlando has fallen in love with Rosalind and wishes to proclaim that to the whole world.

## Act 3, Scene 2

ORLANDO
  Hang there, my verse, in witness of my love;
     And thou, thrice-crownèd queen of night, survey
  With thy chaste eye, from thy pale sphere above,
     Thy huntress' name that my full life doth sway.
  O Rosalind, these trees shall be my books,
     And in their barks my thoughts I'll character
  That every eye which in this forest looks
     Shall see thy virtue witnessed everywhere.
  Run, run, Orlando; carve on every tree
  The fair, the chaste, and unexpressive she.

# A Midsummer Night's Dream

*To the King's Theatre, where we saw* Midsummer Night's Dream, *which I had never seen before, nor shall ever again, for it is the most insipid, ridiculous play that ever I saw in my life!*

Samuel Pepys

Another open-air favourite, *A Midsummer Night's Dream* is thought to have been written in 1594 or 1595. As a poetic drama of exquisite charm, supreme wit and humanity, the play is one of Shakespeare's greatest achievements.

There is seemingly no single source from which the plot was derived. The story of Theseus and Hippolyta could have come from either Chaucer's *Knight's Tale* or Plutarch's *Lives*, and the 'Tragical Comedy' of *Pyramus and Thisbe* is a parody of the tale in Ovid's *Metamorphoses*.

The supernatural element of the play may be based on either folklore or literature; indeed, Shakespeare may well have read about Robin Goodfellow in Reginald Scot's *Discovery of Witchcraft* (1586).

We join the action at a point where Oberon, King of the Fairies, is at daggers drawn with his Queen, Titania. He intends to anoint her eyes with a magic juice which will make her fall in love with the first object she sees when she wakes . . . which turns out to be a man wearing the head of an ass!

## *Act 2, Scene 1*

OBERON

I know a bank where the wild thyme blows,
Where oxlips and the nodding violet grows,
Quite overcanopied with luscious woodbine,
With sweet musk-roses, and with eglantine.
There sleeps Titania sometime of the night,
Lulled in these flowers with dances and delight;
And there the snake throws her enamelled skin,
Weed wide enough to wrap a fairy in;
And with the juice of this I'll streak her eyes,
And make her full of hateful fantasies.
Take thou some of it, and seek through this grove.
A sweet Athenian lady is in love
With a disdainful youth. Anoint his eyes;
But do it when the next thing he espies
May be the lady. Thou shalt know the man
By the Athenian garments he hath on.
Effect it with some care, that he may prove
More fond on her than she upon her love.

. . .

# Sonnet 116

Constancy is the theme of Sonnet 116, at the end of which the poet defies the reader to prove him wrong.

Let me not to the marriage of true minds
Admit impediments. Love is not love
Which alters when it alteration finds,
Or bends with the remover to remove.
O no, it is an ever fixèd mark
That looks on tempests and is never shaken;
It is the star to every wand'ring barque,
Whose worth's unknown although his height be taken.
Love's not time's fool, though rosy lips and cheeks
Within his bending sickle's compass come;
Love alters not with his brief hours and weeks,
But bears it out even to the edge of doom.
   If this be error and upon me proved,
   I never writ, nor no man ever loved.

# Antony and Cleopatra

Based mainly on the life of Marcus Antonius in North's translation of Plutarch's *Lives*, the action of *Antony and Cleopatra* opens in 40 BC, two years after the end of *Julius Caesar*. In this earlier play, Mark Antony had formed a triumvirate with Octavius Caesar and Lepidus, but that has now disintegrated because of his infatuation with Cleopatra, the Queen of Egypt.

Antony is defeated in battle and, believing Cleopatra to be dead, kills himself in despair. When Cleopatra learns that Octavius plans to parade her through the streets of Rome, she decides to join her lover in death rather than undergo such humiliation.

## Act 5, Scene 2

CLEOPATRA

Give me my robe. Put on my crown. I have
Immortal longings in me. Now no more
The juice of Egypt's grape shall moist this lip.
[*Charmian and Iras help her to dress*]
Yare, yare, good Iras, quick – methinks I hear
Antony call. I see him rouse himself
To praise my noble act. I hear him mock
The luck of Caesar, which the gods give men
To excuse their after wrath. Husband, I come.
Now to that name my courage prove my title.
I am fire and air; my other elements
I give to baser life. So, have you done?
Come then, and take the last warmth of my lips.
[*She kisses them*]
Farewell, kind Charmian. Iras, long farewell.
[*Iras falls and dies*]
Have I the aspic in my lips? Dost fall?
If thou and nature can so gently part,
The stroke of death is as a lover's pinch,
Which hurts and is desired. Dost thou lie still?
If thus thou vanishest, thou tell'st the world
It is not worth leave-taking.

CHARMIAN

Dissolve, thick cloud, and rain, that I may say
The gods themselves do weep.

91

CLEOPATRA
    This proves me base.
    If she first meet the curlèd Antony
    He'll make demand of her, and spend that kiss
    Which is my heaven to have.
        [*She takes an aspic from the basket and puts it to
        her breast*]
    Come, thou mortal wretch,
    With thy sharp teeth this knot intrinsicate
    Of life at once untie. Poor venomous fool,
    Be angry, and dispatch. O, couldst thou speak,
    That I might hear thee call great Caesar ass
    Unpolicied!
CHARMIAN
    O eastern star!
CLEOPATRA
    Peace, peace.
    Dost thou not see my baby at my breast,
    That sucks the nurse asleep?
CHARMIAN
    O, break! O, break!
CLEOPATRA
    As sweet as balm, as soft as air, as gentle.
    O Antony!
        [*She puts another aspic to her arm*]
    Nay, I will take thee too.
    What should I stay–
        [*She dies*
CHARMIAN
    In this vile world? So, fare thee well.

Now boast thee, death, in thy possession lies
A lass unparalleled. Downy windows, close,
And golden Phoebus never be beheld
Of eyes again so royal. Your crown's awry.
I'll mend it, and then play—
    [*Enter the Guard, rustling in*]

FIRST GUARD
Where's the Queen?

CHARMIAN
Speak softly. Wake her not.

FIRST GUARD
Caesar hath sent—

CHARMIAN
Too slow a messenger.
    [*She applies an aspic*]
      O come apace, dispatch! I partly feel thee.

FIRST GUARD
Approach, ho! All's not well. Caesar's beguiled.

SECOND GUARD
There's Dolabella sent from Caesar. Call him.
    [*Exit a Guardsman*]

FIRST GUARD
What work is here, Charmian? Is this well done?

CHARMIAN
It is well done, and fitting for a princess
Descended of so many royal kings.
Ah, soldier!
    [*She dies*

# Romeo and Juliet

Romeo and Juliet, those 'star-crossed' lovers in fair Verona, are in fact mere children hardly into their teens, and yet they arrange to be married in secret by Friar Lawrence.

During a street brawl, however, Romeo's friend Mercutio is killed by Juliet's cousin Tybalt. Enraged by this needless death, Romeo kills Tybalt and is banished from Verona.

Blissfully unaware of these events, Juliet waits for night and the return of her lover.

## *Act 3, Scene 2*

JULIET

Gallop apace, you fiery-footed steeds,
Towards Phoebus' lodging. Such a waggoner
As Phaëton would whip you to the west
And bring in cloudy night immediately.
Spread thy close curtain, love-performing night,
That runaways' eyes may wink, and Romeo
Leap to these arms untalked of and unseen.
Lovers can see to do their amorous rites
By their own beauties; or, if love be blind,
It best agrees with night. Come, civil night,
Thou sober-suited matron all in black,
And learn me how to lose a winning match
Played for a pair of stainless maidenhoods.
Hood my unmanned blood, bating in my cheeks,
With thy black mantle till strange love grown bold
Think true love acted simple modesty.
Come night, come Romeo; come, thou day in night,
For thou wilt lie upon the wings of night
Whiter than new snow on a raven's back.
Come, gentle night; come, loving, black-browed night,
Give me my Romeo, and when I shall die
Take him and cut him out in little stars,
And he will make the face of heaven so fine
That all the world will be in love with night
And pay no worship to the garish sun.

O, I have bought the mansion of a love
But not possessed it, and though I am sold,
Not yet enjoyed. So tedious is this day
As is the night before some festival
To an impatient child that hath new robes
And may not wear them.
>    *Enter the Nurse (wringing her hands) with the*
>    *ladder of cords (in her lap)*
O, here comes my Nurse,
And she brings news, and every tongue that speaks
But Romeo's name speaks heavenly eloquence.
Now, Nurse, what news? What, hast thou there
The cords that Romeo bid thee fetch?

NURSE

[*putting down the cords*]
Ay, ay, the cords.

JULIET

Ay me, what news? Why dost thou wring thy hands?

NURSE

Ah, welladay! He's dead, he's dead, he's dead!
We are undone, lady, we are undone.
Alack the day, he's gone, he's killed, he's dead!

JULIET

Can heaven be so envious?

NURSE

Romeo can,
Though heaven cannot. O Romeo, Romeo,
Who ever would have thought it Romeo?

JULIET

What devil art thou that dost torment me thus?

This torture should be roared in dismal hell.
Hath Romeo slain himself? Say thou but 'Ay',
And that bare vowel 'I' shall poison more
Than the death-darting eye of cockatrice.
I am not I if there be such an 'Ay',
Or those eyes shut that make thee answer 'Ay'.
If he be slain, say 'Ay'; or if not, 'No'.
Brief sounds determine of my weal or woe.

# IV

## SOLDIER

Then a soldier,
Full of strange oaths, and bearded like the pard,
Jealous in honour, sudden and quick in quarrel,
Seeking the bubble reputation
Even in the cannon's mouth.

# Henry V

As in *Henry IV*, Parts 1 and 2, Shakespeare obtained much of his source material for this historical work from *The Famous Victories of Henry the Fifth* (1598) and the chronicle histories of Edward Hall (1542) and Holinshed (1577).

Although the play's heroic aspects have made it especially popular in times of war, Shakespeare himself made no attempt to gloss over the horrors of battle.

Shortly after his coronation, Henry decides to press his claim to the French throne and leads his army into battle against a vastly superior force. Of the two speeches that follow, the first, in front of the gates of Harfleur, is one of the most famous rallying cries in all literature, the second before the battle of Agincourt, a promise of pride in years to come for those that stand and face overwhelming odds.

## *Act 3, Scene 1*

KING HARRY

Once more unto the breach, dear friends, once more,
Or close the wall up with our English dead.
In peace there's nothing so becomes a man
As modest stillness and humility,
But when the blast of war blows in our ears,
Then imitate the action of the tiger.
Stiffen the sinews, conjure up the blood,
Disguise fair nature with hard-favoured rage.
Then lend the eye a terrible aspect,
Let it pry through the portage of the head
Like the brass cannon, let the brow o'erwhelm it
As fearfully as doth a gallèd rock
O'erhang and jutty his confounded base,
Swilled with the wild and wasteful ocean.
Now set the teeth and stretch the nostril wide,
Hold hard the breath, and bend up every spirit
To his full height. On, on, you noblest English,
Whose blood is fet from fathers of war-proof,
Fathers that like so many Alexanders
Have in these parts from morn till even fought,
And sheathed their swords for lack of argument.
Dishonour not your mothers; now attest
That those whom you called fathers did beget you.
Be copy now to men of grosser blood,
And teach them how to war. And you, good yeomen,

105

Whose limbs were made in England, show us here
The mettle of your pasture; let us swear
That you are worth your breeding – which I doubt
      not,
For there is none of you so mean and base
That hath not noble lustre in your eyes.
I see you stand like greyhounds in the slips,
Straining upon the start. The game's afoot.
Follow your spirit, and upon this charge
Cry, 'God for Harry! England and Saint George!'

## Act 4, Scene 3

WARWICK
  O that we now had here
  But one ten thousand of those men in England
  That do no work today.
KING HARRY
  What's he that wishes so?
  My cousin Warwick? No, my fair cousin.
  If we are marked to die, we are enough
  To do our country loss; and if to live,
  The fewer men, the greater share of honour.
  God's will, I pray thee wish not one man more.
  By Jove, I am not covetous for gold,
  Nor care I who doth feed upon my cost;
  It ernes me not if men my garments wear;
  Such outward things dwell not in my desires.
  But if it be a sin to covet honour

I am the most offending soul alive.
No, faith, my coz, wish not a man from England.
God's peace, I would not lose so great an honour
As one man more methinks would share from me
For the best hope I have. O do not wish one more.
Rather proclaim it presently through my host
That he which hath no stomach to this fight,
Let him depart. His passport shall be made
And crowns for convoy put into his purse.
We would not die in that man's company
That fears his fellowship to die with us.
This day is called the Feast of Crispian.
He that outlives this day and comes safe home
Will stand a-tiptoe when this day is named
And rouse him at the name of Crispian.
He that shall see this day and live t'old age
Will yearly on the vigil feast his neighbours
And say, 'Tomorrow is Saint Crispian.'
Then will he strip his sleeve and show his scars
And say, 'These wounds I had on Crispin's day.'
Old men forget; yet all shall be forgot,
But he'll remember, with advantages,
What feats he did that day. Then shall our names,
Familiar in his mouth as household words—
Harry the King, Bedford and Exeter,
Warwick and Talbot, Salisbury and Gloucester—
Be in their flowing cups freshly remembered.
This story shall the good man teach his son,
And Crispin Crispian shall ne'er go by
From this day to the ending of the world

But we in it shall be rememberèd,
We few, we happy few, we band of brothers.
For he today that sheds his blood with me
Shall be my brother; be he ne'er so vile,
This day shall gentle his condition.
And gentlemen in England now abed
Shall think themselves accursed they were not here,
And hold their manhoods cheap whiles any speaks
That fought with us upon Saint Crispin's day.

# Sonnet 25

—∽∽—

Our selection from the sonnets continues with no. 25 in which the writer suggests that the security of love is preferable to the short-lived fame of the warrior.

Let those who are in favour with their stars
Of public honour and proud titles boast,
Whilst I, whom fortune of such triumph bars,
Unlooked-for joy in that I honour most.
Great princes' favourites their fair leaves spread
But as the marigold at the sun's eye,
And in themselves their pride lies burièd,
For at a frown they in their glory die.
The painful warrior famousèd for might,
After a thousand victories once foiled
Is from the book of honour razèd quite,
And all the rest forgot for which he toiled.
    Then happy I, that love and am beloved
    Where I may not remove nor be removed.

# Richard III

—◆—

Our final scenes from *Richard III* illustrate the courageous side of his otherwise villainous character.

Richard has imprisoned the late King's two young sons in the Tower of London and has seized power with the help of the Duke of Buckingham. To further strenghthen his position, he orders the murder of the Princes and seeks to marry Elizabeth, daughter of Edward IV.

It is at this time that the representative of the rival House of Lancaster has raised an army, and Richard now faces him at Bosworth Field.

## *Act 5, Scene 6*

*Enter King Richard, Sir Richard Ratcliffe, Sir
William Catesby, and others*

KING RICHARD

What said Northumberland, as touching Richmond?

RATCLIFFE

That he was never trainèd up in arms.

KING RICHARD

He said the truth. And what said Surrey then?

RATCLIFFE

He smiled and said, 'The better for our purpose.'

KING RICHARD

He was in the right, and so indeed it is.

*Clock strikes*

Tell the clock there. Give me a calendar.

Who saw the sun today?

[*A book is brought*]

RATCLIFFE

Not I, my lord.

KING RICHARD

Then he disdains to shine, for by the book

He should have braved the east an hour ago.

A black day will it be to somebody.

Ratcliffe.

RATCLIFFE

My lord?

KING RICHARD

The sun will not be seen today.
The sky doth frown and lour upon our army.
I would these dewy tears were from the ground.
Not shine today – why, what is that to me
More than to Richmond? For the selfsame heaven
That frowns on me looks sadly upon him.
  *Enter the Duke of Norfolk*

NORFOLK
  Arm, arm, my lord! The foe vaunts in the field.
KING RICHARD
  Come, bustle, bustle! Caparison my horse.
    [*Richard arms*]
  Call up Lord Stanley, bid him bring his power.
                                              [*Exit one*

I will lead forth my soldiers to the plain,
And thus my battle shall be orderèd.
My forward shall be drawn out all in length,
Consisting equally of horse and foot,
Our archers placèd strongly in the midst.
John Duke of Norfolk, Thomas Earl of Surrey,
Shall have the leading of this multitude.
They thus directed, we ourself will follow
In the main battle, whose puissance on both
  sides
Shall be well wingèd with our chiefest horse.
This, and Saint George to boot! What think'st thou,
  Norfolk?

NORFOLK
  A good direction, warlike sovereign.
    [*He showeth him a paper*]

This paper found I on my tent this morning.
    [*He reads*]
'Jackie of Norfolk be not too bold,
For Dickon thy master is bought and sold.'

KING RICHARD
  A thing devisèd by the enemy.–
Go, gentlemen, each man unto his charge.
Let not our babbling dreams affright our souls.
Conscience is but a word that cowards use,
Devised at first to keep the strong in awe.
Our strong arms be our conscience; swords, our law.
March on, join bravely! Let us to't, pell mell–
If not to heaven, then hand in hand to hell.
    *His oration to his army*
What shall I say, more than I have inferred?
Remember whom you are to cope withal:
A sort of vagabonds, rascals and runaways,
A scum of Bretons and base lackey peasants,
Whom their o'ercloyèd country vomits forth
To desperate ventures and assured destruction.
You sleeping safe, they bring to you unrest;
You having lands and blessed with beauteous wives,
They would distrain the one, distain the other.
And who doth lead them, but a paltry fellow?
Long kept in Bretagne at our mother's cost;
A milksop; one that never in his life
Felt so much cold as over shoes in snow.
Let's whip these stragglers o'er the seas again,
Lash hence these overweening rags of France,
These famished beggars, weary of their lives,

Who – but for dreaming on this fond exploit–
For want of means, poor rats, had hanged them-
selves.
If we be conquered, let *men* conquer us,
And not these bastard Bretons, whom our fathers
Have in their own land beaten, bobbed, and thumped,
And in record left them the heirs of shame.
Shall these enjoy our lands? Lie with our wives?
Ravish our daughters?
    *Drum afar off*
Hark, I hear their drum.
Fight, gentlemen of England! Fight, bold yeomen!
Draw, archers, draw your arrows to the head!
Spur your proud horses hard, and ride in blood!
Amaze the welkin with your broken staves!
    *Enter a Messenger*
What says Lord Stanley? Will he bring his power?

MESSENGER

My lord, he doth deny to come.

KING RICHARD

Off with young George's head!

NORFOLK

My lord, the enemy is past the marsh.
After the battle let George Stanley die.

KING RICHARD

A thousand hearts are great within my bosom.
Advance our standards! Set upon our foes!
Our ancient word of courage, fair Saint George,
Inspire us with the spleen of fiery dragons.
Upon them! Victory sits on our helms!

## Act 5, Scene 7

*Alarum. Excursions. Enter Sir William Catesby*

CATESBY

[*calling*]

Rescue, my lord of Norfolk! Rescue, rescue!

[*To a soldier*] The King enacts more wonders than a
  man,

Daring an opposite to every danger.

His horse is slain, and all on foot he fights,

Seeking for Richmond in the throat of death.

[*calling*] Rescue, fair lord, or else the day is lost!

*Alarums. Enter King Richard*

KING RICHARD

A horse! A horse! My kingdom for a horse!

CATESBY

Withdraw, my lord. I'll help you to a horse.

KING RICHARD

Slave, I have set my life upon a cast,

And I will stand the hazard of the die.

I think there be six Richmonds in the field.

Five have I slain today, instead of him.

A horse! A horse! My kingdom for a horse!

# Macbeth

As a study in the psychology of evil, *Macbeth* must rank as one of the most compelling dramas ever written. As a challenge to performers, it is Macbeth's neurotic self-absorption and his wife's revelation of her repressed humanity that have fascinated actors for nearly four centuries.

The 'Scottish Play' has now reached the scene where Lady Macbeth must dispel the second thoughts which her soldier husband is having about murdering the King.

## *Act 1, Scene 7*

**LADY MACBETH**

He has almost supped. Why have you left the chamber?

**MACBETH**

Hath he asked for me?

**LADY MACBETH**

Know you not he has?

**MACBETH**

We will proceed no further in this business.
He hath honoured me of late, and I have bought
Golden opinions from all sorts of people,
Which would be worn now in their newest gloss,
Not cast aside so soon.

**LADY MACBETH**

Was the hope drunk
Wherein you dressed yourself? Hath it slept since?
And wakes it now to look so green and pale
At what it did so freely? From this time
Such I account thy love. Art thou afeard
To be the same in thine own act and valour
As thou art in desire? Wouldst thou have that
Which thou esteem'st the ornament of life,
And live a coward in thine own esteem,
Letting 'I dare not' wait upon 'I would',
Like the poor cat i'th' adage?

**MACBETH**

Prithee, peace.

I dare do all that may become a man;
Who dares do more is none.

LADY MACBETH

What beast was't then
That made you break this enterprise to me?
When you durst do it, then you were a man;
And to be more than what you were, you would
Be so much more the man. Nor time nor place
Did then adhere, and yet you would make both.
They have made themselves, and that their fitness
   now
Does unmake you. I have given suck, and know
How tender 'tis to love the babe that milks me.
I would, while it was smiling in my face,
Have plucked my nipple from his boneless gums
And dashed the brains out, had I so sworn
As you have done to this.

MACBETH

If we should fail?

LADY MACBETH

We fail!
But screw your courage to the sticking-place
And we'll not fail. When Duncan is asleep–
Whereto the rather shall his day's hard journey
Soundly invite him – his two chamberlains
Will I with wine and wassail so convince
That memory, the warder of the brain,
Shall be a fume, and the receipt of reason
A limbeck only. When in swinish sleep
Their drenchèd natures lies as in a death,

What cannot you and I not perform upon
Th'unguarded Duncan? What not put upon
His spongy officers, who shall bear the guilt
Of our great quell?

MACBETH

Bring forth men-children only,
For thy undaunted mettle should compose
Nothing but males. Will it not be received,
When we have marked with blood those sleepy two
Of his own chamber and used their very daggers,
That they have done't?

LADY MACBETH

Who dares receive it other,
As we shall make our griefs and clamour roar
Upon his death?

MACBETH

I am settled, and bend up
Each corporal agent to this terrible feat.
Away, and mock the time with fairest show.
False face must hide what the false heart doth know.

# Henry IV, Part I

In an earlier scene from *Henry IV*, Part I, we found Hotspur in rebellious mood. His demands that Mortimer be ransomed have since been refused, and the Percy family now sides with the rebels.

Meanwhile, Prince Hal – the King's son and heir – continues to annoy his father by keeping company with Sir John Falstaff and his band of revellers. When he learns of the uprising, however, Hal takes the field at Shrewsbury where he saves his father's life and kills Hotspur.

Act 5, Scene 1 takes place just before the battle when Falstaff who, on any other occasion would have had you believe he could defeat whole armies single-handed, is in a more reflective and sober frame of mind.

SIR JOHN

Hal, if thou see me down in the battle, and bestride
me, so. 'Tis a point of friendship.

PRINCE HARRY

Nothing but a colossus can do thee that friendship. Say
thy prayers, and farewell.

SIR JOHN

I would 'twere bed-time, Hal, and all well.

PRINCE HARRY

Why, thou owest God a death.

SIR JOHN

'Tis not due yet. I would be loath to pay him before
his day. What need I be so forward with him that calls
not on me? Well, 'tis no matter; honour pricks me on.
Yea, but how if honour prick me off when I come on?
How then? Can honour set-to a leg? No. Or an arm?
No. Or take away the grief of a wound? No. Honour
hath no skill in surgery, then? No. What is honour?
A word. What is in that word 'honour'? What is that
'honour'? Air. A trim reckoning! Who hath it? He that
died o' Wednesday. Doth he feel it? No. Doth he hear
it? No. 'Tis insensible then? Yea, to the dead. But will
it not live with the living? No. Why? Detraction will not
suffer it. Therefore I'll none of it. Honour is a mere
scutcheon. And so ends my catechism.

# Julius Caesar

—m—

*Shakespeare is the greatest blackleg in the business: we are asked to compete with a dramatist who starts with every advantage of prestige, who is sound culture personified, who can demand audiences of schoolchildren to eke out the matinées, and who does not even ask for a royalty for his services.*

J. B. Priestley, writing in the magazine *Encore*, 1956

Like so many writers before and after him, Shakespeare was fascinated by Julius Caesar, the man generally regarded as the greatest ruler in the history of the civilised world.

His interest lay not only in the events leading up to Caesar's death, but also in the subsequent actions of those responsible for it. When Mark Antony discovers Caesar's body, he feigns friendliness towards the conspirators and asks only that he be allowed to speak at the funeral. When he does so, his oration so inflames the people that the assassins are driven out of Rome.

## Act 3, Scene 2

FIRST PLEBEIAN
Stay, ho, and let us hear Mark Antony.

THIRD PLEBEIAN
Let him go up into the public chair.
We'll hear him. Noble Antony, go up.

ANTONY
For Brutus' sake I am beholden to you.
[*Antony ascends to the pulpit*]

[FIFTH] PLEBEIAN
What does he say of Brutus?

THIRD PLEBEIAN
He says, for Brutus' sake
He finds himself beholden to us all.

[FIFTH] PLEBEIAN
'Twere best he speak no harm of Brutus here!

FIRST PLEBEIAN
This Caesar was a tyrant.

THIRD PLEBEIAN
Nay, that's certain.
We are blessed that Rome is rid of him.
[*Enter*] *Antony in the pulpit*

[FOURTH] PLEBEIAN
Peace, let us hear what Antony can say.

ANTONY
You gentle Romans

ALL THE PLEBEIANS
  Peace, ho! Let us hear him.
ANTONY
  Friends, Romans, countrymen, lend me your ears.
  I come to bury Caesar, not to praise him.
  The evil that men do lives after them;
  The good is oft interrèd with their bones.
  So let it be with Caesar. The noble Brutus
  Hath told you Caesar was ambitious.
  If it were so, it was a grievous fault,
  And grievously hath Caesar answered it.
  Here, under leave of Brutus and the rest–
  For Brutus is an honourable man,
  So are they all, all honourable men–
  Come I to speak in Caesar's funeral.
  He was my friend, faithful and just to me.
  But Brutus says he was ambitious,
  And Brutus is an honourable man.
  He hath brought many captives home to Rome,
  Whose ransoms did the general coffers fill.
  Did this in Caesar seem ambitious?
  When that the poor have cried, Caesar hath wept.
  Ambition should be made of sterner stuff.
  Yet Brutus says he was ambitious,
  And Brutus is an honourable man.
  You all did see that on the Lupercal
  I thrice presented him a kingly crown,
  Which he did thrice refuse. Was this ambition?
  Yet Brutus says he was ambitious,
  And sure he is an honourable man.

I speak not to disprove what Brutus spoke,
But here I am to speak what I do know.
You all did love him once, not without cause.
What cause withholds you then to mourn for him?
O judgement, thou art fled to brutish beasts,
And men have lost their reason!
    [*He weeps*]
Bear with me.
My heart is in the coffin there with Caesar,
And I must pause till it come back to me.

FIRST PLEBEIAN
Methinks there is much reason in his sayings.

[FOURTH] PLEBEIAN
If thou consider rightly of the matter,
Caesar has had great wrong.

THIRD PLEBEIAN
Has he not, masters?
I fear there will a worse come in his place.

[FIFTH] PLEBEIAN
Marked ye his words? He would not take the crown,
Therefore 'tis certain he was not ambitious.

FIRST PLEBEIAN
If it be found so, some will dear abide it.

[FOURTH] PLEBEIAN
Poor soul, his eyes are red as fire with weeping.

THIRD PLEBEIAN
There's not a nobler man in Rome than Antony.

# Othello

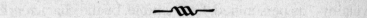

When Shakespeare chose to make his tragic hero Othello a black man, he took an unprecedented step. Until then, blackness had always been associated with sin, death and villainy – as personified, for example, by the character of Aaron in *Titus Andronicus*.

Shakespeare found the story of the Moorish commander tricked into believing that his wife had been unfaithful in Giraldi's *Gli Ecatommiti – The Hundred Tales*. As well as introducing a few characters of his own to the basic tale, Shakespeare added the military action between Turkey and Venice. His information about the Turkish invasion of Cyprus would undoubtedly have come from Richard Knolles' *History of the Turks*, published in 1603.

Othello is a Moorish general in the service of Venice. When he appoints Cassio as his chief lieutenant in preference to his ensign, Iago, the latter seeks revenge. The scheme he devises leads not only to the dismissal of Cassio, but also to Othello murdering his wife Desdemona, and to the suicide of the Moor himself.

Kenneth Tynan, the famous theatre critic of the *Observer*, once wrote: 'I think of *Othello* as a theatrical bullfight, in which the hero is a noble bull, repeatedly charging the handkerchief in the wristy grip of Iago, the dominating Matador.'

In this scene from Act 1, Scene 3, Othello reflects on his early life.

OTHELLO
    Her father loved me, oft invited me,
    Still questioned me the story of my life
    From year to year, the battles, sieges, fortunes
    That I have passed.
    I ran it through even from my boyish days
    To th' very moment that he bade me tell it,
    Wherein I spoke of most disastrous chances,
    Of moving accidents by flood and field,
    Of hair-breadth scapes i'th' imminent deadly breach,
    Of being taken by the insolent foe
    And sold to slavery, of my redemption thence,
    And portance in my traveller's history,
    Wherein of antres vast and deserts idle,
    Rough quarries, rocks, and hills whose heads touch
       heaven,
    It was my hint to speak. Such was my process,
    And of the cannibals that each other eat,
    The Anthropophagi, and men whose heads
    Do grow beneath their shoulders. These things to
       hear
    Would Desdemona seriously incline,
    But still the house affairs would draw her thence,
    Which ever as she could with haste dispatch
    She'd come again, and with a greedy ear
    Devour up my discourse; which I observing,
    Took once a pliant hour, and found good means
    To draw from her a prayer of earnest heart
    That I would all my pilgrimage dilate,
    Whereof by parcels she had something heard,

But not intentively. I did consent,
And often did beguile her of her tears
When I did speak of some distressful stroke
That my youth suffered. My story being done,
She gave me for my pains a world of kisses.
She swore in faith 'twas strange, 'twas passing strange,
'Twas pitiful, 'twas wondrous pitiful.
She wished she had not heard it, yet she wished
That heaven had made her such a man. She thankèd
  me,
And bade me, if I had a friend that loved her,
I should but teach him how to tell my story,
And that would woo her. Upon this hint I spake.
She loved me for the dangers I had passed,
And I loved her that she did pity them.
This only is the witchcraft I have used.

# V

## JUSTICE

—◆—

And then the justice,
In fair round belly with good capon lin'd,
With eyes severe, and beard of formal cut,
Full of wise saws and modern instances;
And so he plays his part.

# The Merchant of Venice

The Stationers' Register of 22 July 1598 has the entry: 'A Book of *The Merchant of Venice* or otherwise called *The Jew of Venice*'. When the work eventually appeared in print in 1600, the title had been changed to *The Comical History of the Merchant of Venice*.

The play is constructed from tales in *Il Pecorone*, a collection of Italian stories published in the sixteenth century. Antonio, a Venetian merchant, borrows money from Shylock, the Jew of the original title, which he is unable to repay. At the subsequent trial, Shylock demands the pound of flesh that was pledged as security.

In the first of our extracts, Shylock maintains that justice should be available to Christian and Jew alike. In the second, Portia, wife of Antonio's friend Bassanio, disguises herself as an advocate and pleads that the justice Shylock seeks should be tempered with mercy.

## Act 3, Scene 1

SHYLOCK

You knew, none so well, none so well as you, of my daughter's flight.

SALERIO

That's certain. I for my part knew the tailor that made the wings she flew withal.

SOLANIO

And Shylock for his own part knew the bird was fledge, and then it is the complexion of them all to leave the dam.

SHYLOCK

She is damned for it.

SALERIO

That's certain, if the devil may be her judge.

SHYLOCK

My own flesh and blood to rebel!

SOLANIO

Out upon it, old carrion, rebels it at these years?

SHYLOCK

I say my daughter is my flesh and my blood.

SALERIO

There is more difference between thy flesh and hers than between jet and ivory; more between your bloods than there is between red wine and Rhenish. But tell us, do you hear whether Antonio have had any loss at sea or no?

SHYLOCK

There I have another bad match. A bankrupt, a prodigal, who dare scarce show his head on the Rialto; a beggar, that was used to come so smug upon the mart. Let him look to his bond. He was wont to call me usurer: let him look to his bond. He was wont to lend money for a Christian courtesy: let him look to his bond.

SALERIO

Why, I am sure if he forfeit thou wilt not take his flesh. What's that good for?

SHYLOCK

To bait fish withal. If it will feed nothing else it will feed my revenge. He hath disgraced me, and hindered me half a million; laughed at my losses, mocked at my gains, scorned my nation, thwarted my bargains, cooled my friends, heated mine enemies, and what's his reason? – I am a Jew. Hath not a Jew eyes? Hath not a Jew hands, organs, dimensions, senses, affections, passions; fed with the same food, hurt with the same weapons, subject to the same diseases, healed by the same means, warmed and cooled by the same winter and summer as a Christian is? If you prick us do we not bleed? If you tickle us do we not laugh? If you poison us do we not die? And if you wrong us shall we not revenge? If we are like you in the rest, we will resemble you in that. If a Jew wrong a Christian, what is his humility? Revenge. If a Christian wrong a Jew, what should his sufferance be by Christian example? Why, revenge. The villainy you teach me I will execute, and it shall go hard but I will better the instruction.

## Act 4, Scene 1

*PORTIA*

The quality of mercy is not strained.
It droppeth as the gentle rain from heaven
Upon the place beneath. It is twice blest:
It blesseth him that gives, and him that takes.
'Tis mightiest in the mightiest. It becomes
The thronèd monarch better than his crown.
His sceptre shows the force of temporal power,
The attribute to awe and majesty,
Wherein doth sit the dread and fear of kings;
But mercy is above this sceptred sway.
It is enthronèd in the hearts of kings;
It is an attribute to God himself,
And earthly power doth then show likest God's
When mercy seasons justice. Therefore, Jew,
Though justice be thy plea, consider this:
That in the course of justice none of us
Should see salvation. We do pray for mercy,
And that same prayer doth teach us all to render
The deeds of mercy. . . .

# King Lear

—m—

*The Lear of Shakespeare cannot be acted. To see Lear acted is to see an old man tottering about the stage with a walking stick, turned out of doors by his daughters on a rainy night.*

Charles Lamb

The 'justice theme' is continued with a further dip into *King Lear*, namely the scene in which the disillusioned monarch tells his daughter Regan how badly he has been treated by her sister.

A delightful anecdote concerning a production of the play is well worth recounting here. The incident took place in Washington DC during the last century when a wheelbarrow full of cannon-balls provided the sound effects during the storm scene. To simulate the roar of thunder, the barrow had to be wheeled over an uneven surface. Striving for a truly deafening rumble one night, an overenthusiastic stagehand upset the barrow, causing two cannon-balls to roll across the stage. The sight of the aged King leaping for his very life with the agility of a ten-year-old was definitely not what Shakespeare had in mind for his audience!

## Act 2, Scene 2

LEAR

Belovèd Regan,
Thy sister's naught. O, Regan, she hath tied
Sharp-toothed unkindness like a vulture here.
I can scarce speak to thee. Thou'lt not believe
With how depraved a quality – O, Regan!

REGAN

I pray you, sir, take patience. I have hope
You less know how to value her desert
Than she to scant her duty.

LEAR

Say, how is that?

REGAN

I cannot think my sister in the least
Would fail her obligation. If, sir, perchance
She have restrained the riots of your followers,
'Tis on such ground and to such wholesome end
As clears her from all blame.

LEAR

My curses on her.

REGAN

O sir, you are old.
Nature in you stands on the very verge
Of his confine. You should be ruled and led
By some discretion that discerns your state
Better than you yourself. Therefore I pray you

That to our sister you do make return;
Say you have wronged her.

LEAR

Ask her forgiveness?
Do you but mark how this becomes the house?
[*Kneeling*] 'Dear daughter, I confess that I am old.
Age is unnecessary. On my knees I beg
That you'll vouchsafe me raiment, bed, and food.'

REGAN

Good sir, no more. These are unsightly tricks.
Return you to my sister.

LEAR

[*rising*]
Never, Regan.
She hath abated me of half my train,
Looked black upon me, struck me with her tongue
Most serpent-like upon the very heart.
All the stored vengeances of heaven fall
On her ingrateful top! Strike her young bones,
You taking airs, with lameness!

CORNWALL

Fie, sir, fie.

LEAR

You nimble lightnings, dart your blinding flames
Into her scornful eyes. Infect her beauty,
You fen-sucked fogs drawn by the pow'rful sun
To fall and blister.

REGAN

O, the blest gods!
So will you wish on me when the rash mood is on.

LEAR

No, Regan. Thou shalt never have my curse.
Thy tender-hafted nature shall not give
Thee o'er to harshness. Her eyes are fierce, but thine
Do comfort and not burn. 'Tis not in thee
To grudge my pleasures, to cut off my train,
To bandy hasty words, to scant my sizes,
And, in conclusion, to oppose the bolt
Against my coming in. Thou better know'st
The offices of nature, bond of childhood,
Effects of courtesy, dues of gratitude.
Thy half o'th' kingdom hast thou not forgot,
Wherein I thee endowed.

# VI

## PANTALOON

—w—

The sixth age shifts
Into the lean and slipper'd pantaloon,
With spectacles on nose and pouch on side,
His youthful hose, well saved, a world too wide
For his shrunk shank; and his big, manly voice,
Turning again towards childish treble, pipes
And whistles in his sound.

# The Passionate Pilgrim

—᪲—

In 1599, the printer William Jaggard published a collection of lyric poems under the title *The Passionate Pilgrim*. Although the book announced that they were 'by W. Shakespeare', only about four of the poems are now considered to be his.

A reprint in 1612 included nine poems by Thomas Heywood who immediately complained of the injury done to him by 'printing his work in a less volume, under the name of another, which may put the world in opinion I might steal them from him . . . But as I must acknowledge my lines not worthy his patronage under whom he hath published them, so the author I know much offended with Master Jaggard that, altogether unknown to him, presumed to make so bold with his name.'

It was probably as a result of this complaint that the original title-page of the 1612 edition was replaced with one that omitted Shakespeare's name.

In verse 12 of the collection, the writer contrasts the freedom of youth with the restrictions of old age.

Crabbèd age and youth cannot live together:
Youth is full of pleasance, age is full of care;
Youth like summer morn, age like winter weather;
Youth like summer brave, age like winter bare.
Youth is full of sport, age's breath is short.
Youth is nimble, age is lame,
Youth is hot and bold, age is weak and cold.
Youth is wild and age is tame.
  Age, I do abhor thee; youth, I do adore thee.
    O my love, my love is young.
  Age, I do defy thee. O sweet shepherd, hie thee,
    For methinks thou stay'st too long.

# The Merry Wives of Windsor

*The Merry Wives of Windsor* is essentially an Elizabethan comedy and the only one that Shakespeare set firmly in England. Many of its details would have been familiar to the Londoners of his day, and the language used is both contemporary and colloquial.

The plot, however, owes little to real life and is more in the tradition of the Italian *novella*. Accordingly, it may well have come from a tale in *Il Pecorone* – a book well known to Shakespeare and one which he turned to for other ideas.

The story pivots around Sir John Falstaff's unsuccessful attempts at seduction, and in Act 3, Scene 5 we find the obese braggart recovering from his amorous adventures. He may not be as 'lean and slippered' as Jaques suggests for man's sixth age but, as this scene proves, is a pantaloon certainly. Recounting his romantic encounter with another man's wife is a risky enough business; recounting it to her husband – who just happens to have disguised himself for the occasion – is courting disaster.

*Enter Sir John Falstaff*

SIR JOHN
Bardolph, I say!
*Enter Bardolph*

BARDOLPH
Here, sir.

SIR JOHN
Go fetch me a quart of sack; put a toast in't.

[*Exit Bardolph*

Have I lived to be carried in a basket like a barrow of butcher's offal, and to be thrown in the Thames? Well, if I be served such another trick, I'll have my brains ta'en out and buttered, and give them to a dog for a New Year's gift. 'Sblood, the rogues slighted me into the river with as little remorse as they would have drowned a blind bitch's puppies, fifteen i'th' litter! And you may know by my size that I have a kind of alacrity in sinking. If the bottom were as deep as hell, I should down. I had been drowned, but that the shore was shelvy and shallow – a death that I abhor, for the water swells a man, and what a thing should I have been when I had been swelled? By the Lord, a mountain of mummy!

*Enter Bardolph, with [two large cups of] sack*

BARDOLPH
Here's Mistress Quickly, sir, to speak with you.

SIR JOHN
Come, let me pour in some sack to the Thames' water, for my belly's as cold as if I had swallowed snowballs for pills to cool the reins.

[*He drinks*]
Call her in.

BARDOLPH

Come in, woman!

*Enter Mistress Quickly*

MISTRESS QUICKLY

[*to Sir John*] By your leave; I cry you mercy. Give your
worship good morrow!

SIR JOHN

[*drinking, then speaking to Bardolph*] Take away these
chalices. Go brew me a pottle of sack, finely.

BARDOLPH

With eggs, sir?

SIR JOHN

Simple of itself. I'll no pullet-sperms in my brewage.

[*Exit Bardolph (with cups)*

How now?

MISTRESS QUICKLY

Marry, sir, I come to your worship from Mistress Ford.

SIR JOHN

Mistress Ford? I have had ford enough: I was thrown
into the ford, I have my belly full of ford.

MISTRESS QUICKLY

Alas the day, good heart, that was not her fault. She does
so take on with her men; they mistook their erection.

SIR JOHN

So did I mine, to build upon a foolish woman's
promise.

MISTRESS QUICKLY

Well, she laments, sir, for it, that it would yearn

your heart to see it. Her husband goes this morning a-birding. She desires you once more to come to her, between eight and nine. I must carry her word quickly. She'll make you amends, I warrant you.

SIR JOHN

Well, I will visit her. Tell her so, and bid her think what a man is; let her consider his frailty, and then judge of my merit.

MISTRESS QUICKLY

I will tell her.

SIR JOHN

Do so. Between nine and ten, sayst thou?

MISTRESS QUICKLY

Eight and nine, sir.

SIR JOHN

Well, be gone. I will not miss her.

MISTRESS QUICKLY

Peace be with you, sir.

SIR JOHN

I marvel I hear not of Master Brooke; he sent me word to stay within. I like his money well.

*Enter Master Ford, disguised as Brooke*

By the mass, here he comes.

FORD

God bless you, sir.

SIR JOHN

Now, Master Brooke, you come to know what hath passed between me and Ford's wife.

FORD

That indeed, Sir John, is my business.

SIR JOHN

Master Brooke, I will not lie to you. I was at her house the hour she appointed me.

FORD

And sped you, sir?

SIR JOHN

Very ill-favouredly, Master Brooke.

FORD

How so, sir? Did she change her determination?

SIR JOHN

No, Master Brooke, but the peaking cornuto her husband, Master Brooke, dwelling in a continual 'larum of jealousy, comes me in the instant of our encounter – after we had embraced, kissed, protested, and, as it were, spoke the prologue of our comedy – and at his heels a rabble of his companions, thither provoked and instigated by his distemper, and, forsooth, to search his house for his wife's love.

FORD

What, while you were there?

SIR JOHN

While I was there.

FORD

And did he search for you, and could not find you?

SIR JOHN

You shall hear. As God would have it, comes in one Mistress Page, gives intelligence of Ford's approach, and, by her invention and Ford's wife's distraction, they conveyed me into a buck-basket–

FORD

A buck-basket?

SIR JOHN

By the Lord, a buck-basket! – rammed me in with foul shirts and smocks, socks, foul stockings, greasy napkins, that, Master Brooke, there was the rankest compound of villainous smell that ever offended nostril.

FORD

And how long lay you there?

SIR JOHN

Nay, you shall hear, Master Brooke, what I have suffered to bring this woman to evil, for your good. Being thus crammed in the basket, a couple of Ford's knaves, his hinds, were called forth by their mistress, to carry me, in the name of foul clothes, to Datchet Lane. They took me on their shoulders, met the jealous knave their master in the door, who asked them once or twice what they had in their basket. I quaked for fear lest the lunatic knave would have searched it, but fate, ordaining he should be a cuckold, held his hand. Well, on went he for a search, and away went I for foul clothes. But mark the sequel, Master Brooke. I suffered the pangs of three several deaths. First, an intolerable fright, to be detected with a jealous rotten bell-wether. Next, to be compassed like a good bilbo in the circumference of a peck, hilt to point, heel to head. And then, to be stopped in, like a strong distillation, with stinking clothes that fretted in their own grease. Think of that – a man of my kidney – think of that – that am as subject to heat as butter, a man of continual dissolution and thaw. It was a miracle to scape suffocation. And in the height of this bath, when I was more than half stewed in grease like a Dutch dish, to be thrown into the Thames and cooled, glowing-hot, in that surge, like a horseshoe. Think of that – hissing hot – think of that, Master Brooke!

# Twelfth Night

The famous lines that open *Twelfth Night* are spoken by
Orsino, the sentimental Duke of Illyria.

## Act 1, Scene 1

ORSINO
   If music be the food of love, play on,
   Give me excess of it that, surfeiting,
   The appetite may sicken and so die.
   That strain again, it had a dying fall.
   O, it came o'er my ear like the sweet sound
   That breathes upon a bank of violets,
   Stealing and giving odour. Enough, no more,
   'Tis not so sweet now as it was before.
      [*Music ceases*]
   O spirit of love, how quick and fresh art thou
   That, notwithstanding thy capacity
   Receiveth as the sea, naught enters there,
   Of what validity and pitch so e'er,
   But falls into abatement and low price
   Even in a minute! So full of shapes is fancy
   That it alone is high fantastical.

Possibly based on a tale from Matteo Bandello's *Novelliere* (1554), the plot of *Twelfth Night* hinges on the confusion caused by the twins Viola and Sebastian, who are separated after a shipwreck, each believing the other to be dead. The title has no particular significance apart from Twelfth Night being, like the play, a time for revelry and generally turning everything upside down.

The consequences of mistaken identity are further complicated by Malvolio, a foolish steward, who secretly aspires to the love of his mistress, Olivia, who eventually marries Sebastian. In Act 2, Scene 5, Malvolio has been given a forged letter which leads him to believe his love is requited.

MALVOLIO

[*taking up the letter*] By my life, this is my lady's hand. These be her very c's, her u's, and her t's, and thus makes she her great P's. It is in contempt of question her hand.

SIR ANDREW

Her c's, her u's, and her t's? Why that?

MALVOLIO

[*reads*] 'To the unknown beloved, this, and my good wishes.' Her very phrases! [*Opening the letter*] By your leave, wax – soft, and the impressure her Lucrece, with which she uses to seal – 'tis my lady. To whom should this be?

FABIAN

This wins him, liver and all.

MALVOLIO

> 'Jove knows I love,
> > But who?
> Lips do not move,
> > No man must know.'

'No man must know.' What follows? The numbers altered. 'No man must know.' If this should be thee, Malvolio?

SIR TOBY

Marry, hang thee, brock.

MALVOLIO

> 'I may command where I adore,
> > But silence like a Lucrece knife
> With bloodless stroke my heart doth gore.
> > M.O.A.I. doth sway my life.'

FABIAN

A fustian riddle.

SIR TOBY

Excellent wench, say I.

MALVOLIO

'M.O.A.I. doth sway my life.' Nay, but first let me see, let me see, let me see.

FABIAN

What dish o'poison has she dressed him!

SIR TOBY

And with what wing the staniel checks at it!

MALVOLIO

'I may command where I adore.' Why, she may command me. I serve her, she is my lady. Why, this is evident to any formal capacity. There is no obstruction in this. And the end – what should that alphabetical

position portend? If I could make that resemble something in me. Softly – 'M.O.A.I.'

SIR TOBY

O ay, make up that, he is now at a cold scent.

FABIAN

Sowter will cry upon't for all this, though it be as rank
as a fox.

MALVOLIO

'M.' Malvolio – 'M' – why, that begins my name.

FABIAN

Did I not say he would work it out? The cur is excellent
at faults.

MALVOLIO

'M.' But then there is no consonancy in the sequel.
That suffers under probation. 'A' should follow, but
'O' does.

FABIAN

And 'O' shall end, I hope.

SIR TOBY

Ay, or I'll cudgel him, and make him cry 'O!'

MALVOLIO

And then 'I' comes behind.

FABIAN

Ay, an you had any eye behind you you might see more
detraction at your heels than fortunes before you.

MALVOLIO

'M.O.A.I.' This simulation is not as the former, and yet
to crush this a little, it would bow to me, for every
one of these letters are in my name. Soft, here follows
prose: 'If this fall into thy hand, revolve. In my stars I

am above thee, but be not afraid of greatness. Some are born great, some achieve greatness, and some have greatness thrust upon 'em. Thy fates open their hands, let thy blood and spirit embrace them, and to inure thyself to what thou art like to be, cast thy humble slough, and appear fresh. Be opposite with a kinsman, surly with servants. Let thy tongue tang arguments of state; put thyself into the trick of singularity. She thus advises thee that sighs for thee. Remember who commended thy yellow stockings, and wished to see thee ever cross-gartered. I say remember, go to, thou art made if thou desirest to be so; if not, let me see thee a steward still, the fellow of servants, and not worthy to touch Fortune's fingers. Farewell. She that would alter services with thee,

The Fortunate-Unhappy.'

Daylight and champaign discovers not more. This is open. I will be proud, I will read politic authors, I will baffle Sir Toby, I will wash off gross acquaintance, I will be point-device the very man. I do not now fool myself, to let imagination jade me; for every reason excites to this, that my lady loves me. She did commend my yellow stockings of late, she did praise my leg, being cross-gartered, and in this she manifests herself to my love, and with a kind of injunction drives me to these habits of her liking. I thank my stars, I am happy. I will be strange, stout, in yellow stockings, and cross-gartered, even with the swiftness of putting on. Jove and my stars be praised. Here is yet a postscript. 'Thou canst not choose but know who I am. If thou entertainest my love, let it appear in thy smiling, thy smiles become thee well. Therefore in my presence still smile, dear my sweet, I prithee.' Jove, I thank thee. I will smile, I will do everything that thou wilt have me.

# Sonnet 22

The comparison between youth and old age is a recurring theme in the Sonnets, and in no. 22 the author looks in the mirror for a glimpse of the truth.

My glass shall not persuade me I am old
So long as youth and thou are of one date;
But when in thee time's furrows I behold,
Then look I death my days should expiate.
For all that beauty that doth cover thee
Is but the seemly raiment of my heart,
Which in thy breast doth live, as thine in me;
How can I then be elder than thou art?
O therefore, love, be of thyself so wary
As I, not for myself, but for thee will,
Bearing thy heart, which I will keep so chary
As tender nurse her babe from faring ill.
    Presume not on thy heart when mine is slain:
    Thou gav'st me thine not to give back again.

# Henry IV, Part II

As in *Henry IV*, Part 1, Shakespeare relies mainly on *The Famous Victories of Henry the Fifth*, Holinshed's *Chronicles* and Samuel Daniel's *Four Books of the Civil Wars* for his source material. Unlike its predecessor, however, this play contains a greater proportion of non-historical material which Shakespeare would probably have invented.

At the end of Part 1 Prince Harry, having spent most of his time with Falstaff's band of revellers, had seemingly seen the error of his dissolute ways. Now he appears to have regressed, although he actually spends less time with Sir John than was previously the case. In fact, it is the knight himself who is more often to be found in the company of Mistress Quickly and Doll Tearsheet at the Boar's Head Tavern in Eastcheap and, later, in Gloucestershire on his way to and from the place of battle.

When Hal is named King, however, it is the more mature and newly crowned Henry V who rejects Falstaff and all he stands for.

## Act 5, Scene 5

*Enter King Harry the Fifth, Prince John of Lancaster,*
*the Dukes of Clarence and Gloucester, the Lord*
*Chief Justice (and others)*

SIR JOHN

God save thy grace, King Hal, my royal Hal!

PISTOL

The heavens thee guard and keep, most royal imp
of fame!

SIR JOHN

God save thee, my sweet boy!

KING HARRY

My Lord Chief Justice, speak to that vain man.

LORD CHIEF JUSTICE

[*to Sir John*]

Have you your wits? Know you what 'tis you speak?

SIR JOHN

My king, my Jove, I speak to thee, my heart!

KING HARRY

I know thee not, old man. Fall to thy prayers.
How ill white hairs becomes a fool and jester!
I have long dreamt of such a kind of man,
So surfeit-swelled, so old, and so profane;
But being awake, I do despise my dream.
Make less thy body hence, and more thy grace.
Leave gormandizing; know the grave doth gape

179

For thee thrice wider than for other men.
Reply not to me with a fool-born jest.
Presume not that I am the thing I was,
For God doth know, so shall the world perceive,
That I have turned away my former self;
So will I those that kept me company.
When thou dost hear I am as I have been,
Approach me, and thou shalt be as thou wast,
The tutor and the feeder of my riots.
Till then I banish thee, on pain of death,
As I have done the rest of my misleaders,
Not to come near our person by ten mile.
For competence of life I will allow you,
That lack of means enforce you not to evils;
And as we hear you do reform yourselves,
We will, according to your strengths and qualities,
Give you advancement. [*To Lord Chief Justice*] Be it
    your charge, my lord,
To see performed the tenor of our word. [*To his train*]
    Set on!

# VII

## SECOND CHILDISHNESS

—m—

Last scene of all,
That ends this strange eventful history,
Is second childishness, and mere oblivion,
Sans teeth, sans eyes, sans taste, sans everything.

# King Lear

—◆—

Our first contribution to the seventh age of man – that of childishness in old age – is a further scene from *King Lear*.

The faithful Cordelia has been disinherited and, although she has no dowry, the King of France has taken her for his wife. When she learns of her father's madness, Cordelia brings over an army from France to Britain, and her two sisters, Goneril and Regan, join forces to counter this threat.

Before the inevitable battle, Cordelia and her father are reunited.

\*

*What I want to say is Shakespeare's model is inadequate now, it just does not work. Acceptance is not enough. Anybody can accept. You can go quietly into your gas chamber . . . You can sit quietly at home and have an H-bomb dropped on you. Shakespeare had time. But time has speeded up enormously, and for us, time is running out . . .*

Edward Bond on his version of the Lear story

## Act 4, Scene 6

CORDELIA

O my dear father, restoration hang
Thy medicine on my lips, and let this kiss
Repair those violent harms that my two sisters
Have in thy reverence made!

KENT

Kind and dear princess!

CORDELIA

Had you not been their father, these white flakes
Did challenge pity of them. Was this a face
To be opposed against the warring winds?
Mine enemy's dog, though he had bit me, should
have stood
That night against my fire. And wast thou fain, poor
father,
To hovel thee with swine and rogues forlorn
In short and musty straw? Alack, alack,
'Tis wonder that thy life and wits at once
Had not concluded all! [*To the Gentleman*] He wakes.
Speak to him.

[FIRST] GENTLEMAN

Madam, do you; 'tis fittest.

CORDELIA

[*to Lear*]
How does my royal lord? How fares your majesty?

LEAR

You do me wrong to take me out o'th' grave.
Thou art a soul in bliss, but I am bound
Upon a wheel of fire, that mine own tears
Do scald like molten lead.

CORDELIA

Sir, do you know me?

LEAR

You are a spirit, I know. Where did you die?

CORDELIA

[*to the Gentleman*]
Still, still far wide!

[FIRST] GENTLEMAN

He's scarce awake. Let him alone a while.

LEAR

Where have I been? Where am I? Fair daylight?
I am mightily abused. I should ev'n die with pity
To see another thus. I know not what to say.
I will not swear these are my hands. Let's see:
I feel this pin prick. Would I were assured
Of my condition.

CORDELIA

[*kneeling*]
O look upon me, sir,
And hold your hands in benediction o'er me.
You must not kneel.

LEAR

Pray do not mock.
I am a very foolish, fond old man,
Fourscore and upward,
Not an hour more nor less; and to deal plainly,

I fear I am not in my perfect mind.
Methinks I should know you, and know this man;
Yet I am doubtful, for I am mainly ignorant
What place this is; and all the skill I have
Remembers not these garments; nor I know not
Where I did lodge last night. Do not laugh at me,
For as I am a man, I think this lady
To be my child, Cordelia.

CORDELIA
And so I am, I am.

LEAR
Be your tears wet? Yes, faith. I pray, weep not.
If you have poison for me, I will drink it.
I know you do not love me; for your sisters
Have, as I do remember, done me wrong.
You have some cause; they have not.

CORDELIA
No cause, no cause.

LEAR
Am I in France?

KENT
In your own kingdom, sir.

LEAR
Do not abuse me.

[FIRST] GENTLEMAN
Be comforted, good madam. The great rage
You see is killed in him. Desire him to go in.
Trouble him no more till further settling.

CORDELIA
[*to Lear*]

Will't please your highness walk?

**LEAR**

You must bear with me. Pray you now, forget
And forgive. I am old and foolish.

# Sonnet 123

—ɯɯ—

Even the inevitability of death does not detract from the poet's appreciation of the riches of old age in Sonnet 123.

No, time, thou shalt not boast that I do change!
Thy pyramids built up with newer might
To me are nothing novel, nothing strange,
They are but dressings of a former sight.
Our dates are brief, and therefore we admire
What thou dost foist upon us that is old,
And rather make them born to our desire
Than think that we before have heard them told.
Thy registers and thee I both defy,
Not wond'ring at the present nor the past;
For thy records and what we see doth lie,
Made more or less by thy continual haste.
    This I do vow, and this shall ever be:
    I will be true despite thy scythe and thee.

# Henry VIII (All is True)

—✠—

There is considerable evidence to suggest that *Henry VIII* was written by Shakespeare in collaboration with John Fletcher (1579–1625).

Two facts, however, are not in dispute. Firstly, the play was originally known as *All is True*, and it was not until it came to be printed as the last of the English history plays that it was given the title *The Famous History of the Life of King Henry the Eighth*.

Secondly, the firing of a cannon during a performance of *All is True* at the Globe Theatre on 29 June 1613 ignited the thatch and burned the building to the ground. Sir Henry Wotton later wrote of the occasion: 'Nothing did perish but wood and straw and a few forsaken cloaks; only one man has his breeches set on fire, that would perhaps have broiled him, if he had not by the benefit of a provident wit put it out with bottle ale.'

The drama begins with the return of Henry VIII from the Field of the Cloth of Gold. The Duke of Buckingham is about to warn the King of the growing power of Cardinal Wolsey when he is falsely accused of treason and executed. Through Wolsey, Henry starts negotiations with the Pope for divorce, but when the Cardinal discovers his true intentions he, too, is accused of treason.

In Act 3, Scene 2, Wolsey reflects on the events that are about to lead to his arrest.

CARDINAL WOLSEY
 So farewell – to the little good you bear me.
 Farewell, a long farewell, to all my greatness!
 This is the state of man. Today he puts forth
 The tender leaves of hopes; tomorrow blossoms,
 And bears his blushing honours thick upon him;
 The third day comes a frost, a killing frost,
 And when he thinks, good easy man, full surely
 His greatness is a-ripening, nips his root,
 And then he falls, as I do. I have ventured,
 Like little wanton boys that swim on bladders,
 This many summers in a sea of glory,
 But far beyond my depth; my high-blown pride
 At length broke under me, and now has left me
 Weary, and old with service, to the mercy
 Of a rude stream that must for ever hide me.
 Vain pomp and glory of this world, I hate ye!
 I feel my heart new opened. O, how wretched
 Is that poor man that hangs on princes' favours!
 There is betwixt that smile we would aspire to,
 That sweet aspect of princes, and their ruin,
 More pangs and fears than wars or women have,
 And when he falls, he falls like Lucifer,
 Never to hope again.

# Sonnet 71

In our final sonnet, no. 71, the poet gives some timely advice to his loved one . . .

No longer mourn for me when I am dead
Than you shall hear the surly sullen bell
Give warning to the world that I am fled
From this vile world with vilest worms to dwell.
Nay, if you read this line, remember not
The hand that writ it; for I love you so
That I in your sweet thoughts would be forgot
If thinking on me then should make you woe.
O, if, I say, you look upon this verse
When I perhaps compounded am with clay,
Do not so much as my poor name rehearse,
But let your love even with my life decay,
    Lest the wise world should look into your moan
    And mock you with me after I am gone.

# The Tempest

Just as Prospero's speech brings down the curtain on the revels in *The Tempest*, so it ends our selection of speeches and scenes that have illustrated Shakespeare's seven ages of man.

Perhaps it would also be appropriate to quote one of Miranda's lines from the same play – a thought that was possibly in the poet's mind when he created so many wonderful characters for us to enjoy:

'How beauteous mankind is! O brave new world
That has such people in't!'

## *Act 4, Scene 1*

PROSPERO

. . .

Our revels now are ended. These our actors,
As I foretold you, were all spirits, and
Are melted into air, into thin air;
And like the baseless fabric of this vision,
The cloud-capped towers, the gorgeous palaces,
The solemn temples, the great globe itself,
Yea, all which it inherit, shall dissolve;
And, like this insubstantial pageant faded,
Leave not a rack behind. We are such stuff
As dreams are made on, and our little life
Is rounded with a sleep. . . .

# Index of Plays

—m—

# List of Poems and Sonnets

—᜖—

*Now available on cassette and CD*

CLASSIC FM FAVOURITE SHAKESPEARE

Performed by Alan Cox, Richard Griffiths, Derek Jacobi, Victoria Hamilton, Antony Sher, Imogen Stubbs

Introduced by John Brunning

On this audio an outstanding cast perform the pieces selected by the readers of *Classic FM Magazine* in the poll to discover their favourite Shakespeare scene, speech or sonnet. This collection, which also includes many additional passages, takes us through the Seven Ages of Man so eloquently described by Jaques in *As You Like It* – Infant and Schoolboy, Lover, Soldier, Justice, Fool and the Second Childishness of old age – and traces how these aspects of human kind are portrayed in Shakespeare's work.

There are extracts from *Richard III, Henry IV, King Lear, Hamlet, Coriolanus, Macbeth, Romeo and Juliet, The Taming of the Shrew, As You like It, A Midsummer Night's Dream, Antony and Cleopatra, The Merchant of Venice, Julius Caesar, Henry V, The Merry Wives of Windsor* and *Henry VIII*, as well as a number of well known sonnets.

With music of the period and introductions to each piece explaining context and background by Classic FM's John Brunning, *Favourite Shakespeare* is a delight, whether you are familiar with the works of Shakespeare or are coming to his glorious poetry afresh.

*To be published in November 1998*

THE CLASSIC FM BOOK OF MUSICAL ANECDOTES,
NOTES AND QUOTES

Henry Kelly and John Foley
Foreword by Lesley Garrett

'Musical people are so absurdly unreasonable. They always want one to be perfectly dumb at the very moment when one is longing to be absolutely deaf.' *Oscar Wilde*

'I spend up to six hours a day waving my arms about, and if everyone else did the same they would stay much healthier.' *Sir Malcolm Sargent*

'People are wrong when they say that opera is not what it used to be. It *is* what it used to be. That is what is wrong with it.' *Noel Coward*

Henry Kelly and John Foley have compiled a rich symphony of anecdotes, notes and quotes from the world of classical music – composers, conductors, soloists, instruments, and their critics – from batons to Beethoven, maracas to *Meistersinger*, Verdi to violas, with an entertaining preface by celebrated singer Lesley Garrett.

*To be published in September 1998*

CLASSIC ROMANCE

A Collection of Writing from the Heart

Nick Bailey

A celebration of Classic FM's most popular programme, *Classic Romance.*

Presenter Nick Bailey has chosen a selection of classic romantic writing, illuminated by the words of Classic FM listeners themselves. For more than five years listeners have been entranced to hear people's romantic encounters read out on the air: now Nick Bailey has selected some of the gems from the thousands of letters he has received. The combination of these stories, together with some of the greatest love poems and love letters ever written, make this a collection to treasure.

*An audio cassette and CD to accompany this book will be produced by Hodder Headline Audiobooks.*

*Already Available*


## CLASSIC FM ONE HUNDRED FAVOURITE POEMS


Introduction and biographies of the poets by Mike Read.

Here are the works chosen by Classic FM listeners in the poll to discover their favourite poems. This is a rich and varied collection: here are not only the famous poems you would expect to find – and all the famous poets – but also some wonderful less well-known works, together with biographies of all the poets by Mike Read.

Includes work by Betjeman, Kipling, Shakespeare, Tennyson, Yeats, Wordsworth, Hardy, Larkin, Brooke, Keats, Auden, Rossetti, Browning, Hopkins, Housman, Burns, Donne, Milton, Masefield, Frost and many others.

*An audio tape and CD to accompany this book are produced by Hodder Headline Audiobooks.*